DILEMMAS
IN THE
CONSULTING ROOM

DILEMMAS
IN THE
CONSULTING ROOM

edited by

Helen Alfillé and Judy Cooper

KARNAC
LONDON   NEW YORK

First published in 2002 by
H. Karnac (Books) Ltd.
6 Pembroke Buildings, London NW10 6RE
A subsidiary of Other Press LLC, New York

British Library Cataloging in Publication Data

A C.I.P. record for this book is available from the British Library.

   ISBN 1 85575 268 9

10 9 8 7 6 5 4 3 2

Edited, designed, and produced by The Studio Publishing Services Ltd, Exeter

Printed in Great Britain by
Biddles Ltd., *www.biddles.co.uk*

"... life's uncertain voyage ..."

"... nothing brings me all things."

SHAKESPEARE: *Timon of Athens* Act V, scene i

CONTENTS

CONTRIBUTORS

Helen Alfillé
Member of the British Association of Psychotherapists. In private practice in London. Co-editor: *Assessment in Psychotherapy* (London: Karnac Books, 1998).

Simon Archer
Member of the British Association of Psychotherapists. In private practice near York. He is a founder member of the North of England Association for Training in Psychoanalytic Psychotherapy, for which he is a training therapist and supervisor.

Ruth Berkowitz PhD
Member of the British Association of Psychotherapists (Adult and Adolescent). Family Therapist (Tavistock Clinic). In private practice in London. Has published in several professional journals and books.

A. H. Brafman MRCPsych
Member of the British Psycho-Analytical Society and a psychoanalyst of adults and children. Has worked in the NHS as a

child and adolescent psychiatrist. Currently Honorary Senior Lecturer in the Psychotherapy Department of University College Hospital, London. Author: *Untying the Knot: Working with Children and Parents* (London: Karnac Books, 2001).

Judy Cooper
Member of the British Association of Psychotherapists. In private practice in London. Author: *Speak of Me as I Am: The Life and Work of Masud Khan* (London: Karnac Books, 1993). Co-editor: *Narcissistic Wounds:Clinical perspectives* (London: Whurr Publishers, 1995). Co-editor: *Assessment in Psychotherapy* (London: Karnac Books, 1998).

Lou Corner
Member of the British Association of Psychotherapists. In private practice in Berkshire. Teaches and runs clinical groups and was Director of Counselling Courses, Reading University.

Dianne Campbell Lefevre MRCP FRCPsych
Consultant psychiatrist in psychotherapy and Honorary Fellow Anglia Polytechnic University. As a consultant psychiatrist has had long experience of treating psychotic patients combining psychological and biological treatments. Currently running the MSc course in the Psychodynamics of the Psychoses, which has a clinical component. Leads workshops on working with borderline and psychotic patients.

Susan Lipshitz-Phillips
Clinical psychologist and Adult psychotherapist trained at the Tavistock Clinic. Member of the British Association of Psychotherapists. In private practice in London. Previously worked at the Camden Psychotherapy Unit. Has lectured on psychoanalytic theory at Universities in England and South Africa. Has published in several books and journals.

Peter Shoenberg MRCP FRCPsych
Member of the British Association of Psychotherapists. Consultant psychotherapist at University College London Hospitals Trust. Honorary Senior Clinical Lecturer at the Royal Free and University College School of Medicine. Has written many papers on

psychotherapy and psychosomatic medicine. Also in private practice in London.

Denise Taylor
Fellow of the British Association of Psychotherapists. Previously worked in the Tavistock Clinic as clinician and tutor. Founder member of the British Confederation of Psychotherapists. Currently in private practice in London.

Daniel Twomey
Member of the British Association of Psychotherapists. Has published in books and journals. In private practice in London.

Mary Twyman
Member of the British Psycho-Analytical Society. In private practice in London.

Anne Tyndale
Member of the British Association of Psychotherapists, where she is also a training therapist and supervisor. In private practice in Brighton. Has published in several books and journals.

Introduction

Helen Alfillé and Judy Cooper

We work in a solitary profession. After rigorous and intensive training, involving a high degree of interaction with an analyst, supervisors and teachers and easy access to sharing with a peer group, suddenly one finds oneself alone. In private practice this can be highly anxiety provoking and may lead to a profound sense of isolation. The therapist needs to put thought and energy into the creation of new links within which he can share experiences, difficulties, anxieties and dilemmas with fellow practitioners. It is not for nothing that rumour has it that it takes 10 years after qualifying to become a competent psychotherapist.

This book is not so much for reference but a guide and a spur which we hope therapists can use to explore and develop their own clinical style within a holding framework. Even the most experienced therapist can be faced with dilemmas and feel uncertain in what is normally a familiar, boundaried setting. Despite this constant structure, psychoanalytic therapy involves a *relationship* between two people and is therefore bound to lead to unique communication based on feelings emerging from the transference and countertransference. For the most part, psychoanalytic literature

1

offers plenty on theory and technique, but little on the detail of mutual clinical exchanges in the consulting room.

Psychoanalysis, in its early days, was a much more informal affair. As it became more widespread and accepted, so it became somewhat institutionalised and more rigid. Perhaps this has not been conducive to acknowledging and exploring some of the more sensitive problems we meet as clinicians. Would Freud have found it problematic to shake a patient's hand? Today we seem to need to debate it.

The possible range of such clinical exchanges is, of course, infinite and could include apparently *practical matters*, such as the setting, money, breaks; *emotional responses* of crying, laughing, dreams and silence; *reflections* on the therapeutic relationship, extending to *less common experiences*, such as violence, psychosis and suicide. To cover all these subjects is, of course, impossible within the confines of one book. We have selected some of them that represent a cross section of issues raised by working psychoanalytic clinicians; but others are no less important. We hope this book will engender further interest in our clinical experiences and shared discussion with colleagues. Perhaps this can be a forum allowing us as therapists to be critical of our own technique and responses in a facilitating environment.

The papers in this book are based on individual work with adults, whether in private practice or, in some cases, in an institution. Some dilemmas are universal, but there is never an absolute answer. We must all develop a style of working within which we feel most comfortable, while holding to the basic tenets of psychoanalysis: the unconscious, transference (and countertransference) and the core importance of early object relationships.

Today, psychoanalysis has become very much a part of the cultural fibre of our times and lay people, having an awareness of its potential, are more demanding in their expectations of psychotherapy, if deciding to enter treatment. As the patient population has broadened considerably and now includes many who would not have been deemed suitable in Freud's day, such as those with narcissistic disorder, borderline personality disorder, addictions and so forth, some of the more rigid styles of the orthodox second generation analysts become open to question. There is nothing to equal the insight that may be gained through the psychoanalytic process, which can lead to fundamental psychic change. However, to follow the technique blindly, with no awareness of the altering social norms, runs the risk of, at worst, psychoanalysis being completely marginalised and at best, having little influence as a form of treatment, rather than maintaining its position in the forefront of the therapeutic world.

With this in mind, we have included papers covering those issues invariably encountered in the consulting room, such as the setting, money, breaks, termination; others highlighting particularly difficult areas of work, such as shame in relation to violence; psychosis and suicide. Yet others describe personal ways of thinking about the therapeutic relationship.

Fundamental to any therapeutic endeavour is the constancy of the setting, allowing space for trust to develop. Susan Lipshitz Phillips argues the need to provide containment and safety so that creative therapeutic work can take place. In her paper, Ruth Berkowitz questions the responses to the therapist's laughter. Is it invariably defensive or can it be a therapeutic and positive factor in the work? The interdependency of psyche and soma is explored by Peter Shoenberg, who stresses the importance of physical symptoms in the patient's communications. Frequently we see that the conflicts of a patient's inner world are manifested through the body. The patient's use of money, both symbolically and in reality, is an essential part of the therapeutic relationship in private practice. Denise Taylor writes about the multiple, sometimes tortuous, projections attached to money brought by patients into the treatment situation. Psychoanalytic therapy could be said to be predicated on separation anxiety and loss. Helen Alfillé explores how one of the basic aims of treatment is to help the patient to internalise a good object, gradually enabling him to separate and become more independent. The ultimate separation in therapy comes with termination and the vicissitudes of ending for both patient and analyst are described by Mary Twyman. She shows how the transference evolves throughout treatment and alters at the end, posing the question of whether it is ever fully resolved. What happens in the internal worlds of patient and therapist at the conclusion of this long intense relationship called psychoanalytic psychotherapy?

Some problems appear insurmountable in the psychotherapeutic process but with current developments in theoretical and technical understanding, clinical boundaries have expanded and analytic work can proceed with particularly difficult patients. Simon Archer explores the shame behind violent and aggressive behaviour as manifested in the transference and demonstrates how it can be used as a force for change. Diane Lefevre emphasises the dangers of missing possible psychotic aspects of a patient. She stresses the importance of careful assessment diagnosis, particularly with regard to differentiating between the psychotic and nonpsychotic aspects of the patient. She describes how the therapist can use psychoanalytic concepts as part of long term treatment in a hospital setting. A. H. Brafman talks of the difficulties in assessing potentially suicidal patients and makes us acutely aware of the need to identify them in terms of those who have a suicidal phantasy and those who are a real suicidal risk.

In compiling this book, it was interesting to observe different clinical approaches to our work despite fundamentally shared theoretical concepts. Daniel Twomey's personal thoughts about what defines him as a psychotherapist and what sustains him in his work, demonstrate how invaluable his intensive training has been, in retaining a firm sense of psychoanalytic identity while allowing him to take a more lateral approach. There are many ways of hearing the patient's story, which affects the therapist's countertransference response. In Anne Tyndale's paper, this response is explored in some detail and she demonstrates her conviction that the therapist must accept the patient's repetition compulsion until he can take responsibility for his own history and effect some psychic change.

A particular predicament met by Lou Corner is one concerning issues of technique in the early stages of treatment when patients who use excessive projective identification present others as the focus in the consulting room, thereby creating confusion as to their real identity. Judy Cooper stresses the importance of maintaining a human dimension in psychotherapeutic work. The relationship, both real and transferential is paramount, and underpinned by the clinical, technical and theoretical considerations, must be contained within the strict parameters of the setting.

We hope this book will be seen as a small part of that tradition of learning from mutual exchange, which includes supervision, scientific meetings, workshops, conferences, lectures, books and papers. Psychoanalysis is constantly evolving and the current emphasis on transference and countertransference interpretation, as well as the range and depth of other dimensions of the therapeutic relationship, make additional demands on the therapist, requiring more from the clinical interaction. This can leave the therapist feeling vulnerable, no longer able to take refuge in a passive stance; for example, in the analytic silence. But it also affords exciting opportunities to provide the patient with a basis for growth and psychic change within the framework of an alive, creative therapeutic relationship.

In the interests of confidentiality, any descriptions of patients that could be recognised have been changed. Any likeness is purely coincidental.

CHAPTER ONE

Some thoughts on the use of the setting in psychoanalytic psychotherapy

Susan Lipshitz-Phillips

P sychoanalytic psychotherapy is predicated on the idea that we cannot be outside our own history. The work of understanding how we are unconsciously directed by it and what change is possible, occurs in a very particular setting. It is this notion of "the setting" that I will be discussing.

Generally, psychoanalytic therapy involves patient and therapist meeting on a regular basis, in the same place for 50-minute sessions from once to five times a week. There are predictable holiday breaks and fees are negotiated and reviewed. It is only in this way that stability is created behaviourally, providing an unvarying background against which the thoughts and actions of the patient and therapist can be understood.

In his book on technique, Etchegoyen (1991) discusses the problem of distinguishing the analytic situation and setting from the analytic process since they influence one another in a dialectic way. He suggests that the "mental attitude" of the analyst is a substantial part of the setting, following Freud who said in 1912, "the doctor should be opaque to his patients and, like a mirror, should show them nothing but what is shown to him" (p. 118), or in other imagery, "he must turn his own unconscious like a receptive organ towards the transmitting unconscious of the patient" (p. 115). Etchegoyen says that the analyst cultivates a reserve and resists gratifying the demands of the patient in order to observe the transference; the reawakening of past object relationships in the present. The same method applies in psychoanalytic psychotherapy.

These special conditions therefore provide the space for infantile desires and phantasies of the patient to manifest themselves, be observed and contained (Bion, 1962) by the presence of the therapist. For the therapist is more than a mirror and his/her own mental state, training and personal therapy have a crucial impact on the setting, themes that I shall return to later on in this chapter.

The historical development of thinking about the setting as a holding space has a parallel with the development of our understanding of the power of unconscious forces. Glover (1955) says, "Freud compared the relation of the ego to the id with that of a rider astride a horse ... James Glover used to say that the attitude of the analyst to his patient should be that of an onlooker who sees a baby perched on an elephant, trying to convince itself that it is master of the situation, yet compelled to give terrified acquiescence to any change of direction initiated by the more powerful locomotive force beneath it". In his early work with Breuer, treating hysterics (1893), Freud came to realise that the suffering patient crying out for help was hindered or interfered with by other unconscious agenda. While psychoanalysts gradually realised that this resistance could be useful to the therapeutic process, they were at first surprised at how the offer of treatment affected their relationship with their patients. They had discovered ambivalence and that there are secondary gains from being ill that were not always easy to give up—some of the locomotive forces Glover mentions. When Freud wrote about the problems of treating hysteria, using the cathartic method of discharging the anxieties associated with pathogenic memories, first trying hypnosis and later abandoning it for talking, he noted how, "fresh symptoms took the place of ones which had been got rid of" [1893, p. 261]. So the unconscious was seen as a large reservoir of active psychic forces from the start.

By the time Freud moved from research to setting up in practice and wrote about his patients illustrating the functioning of the unconscious mind with his case histories, the idea that there were other parts of the mind was not new. Ellenberger (1970) put the development of psychoanalysis into the context of a long history of the development of dynamic psychiatry. He sees a continuum between primitive healing and philosophies and later therapeutic methods. However, I think it was particularly Freud's sustained study and reporting of the influence of therapy on the patient and on the therapist, his theory of psychic states and the development of technique, that created a radical therapy in psychoanalysis and psychotherapy proper.

As their work revealed ever new aspects of the treatment situation, as well as of mental life, Freud and Breuer came, often painfully, to the realisation that their professional interest in their patients produced unexpected effects. For example, Breuer broke off Anna O's treatment when he realised that she was mistaking his attentions towards her. And, with the benefit of hindsight, it seems that Freud, usually so brilliant a sleuth, missed something when he did not realise that he was being referred to in Dora's dreams of a cigar-smoking man. He could trace the figure to her hidden feelings for her father and the family friend Herr K, but took it no further at this stage in his work. In terms of the setting of these treatments, it seems probable that the entry of their doctors into these womens' bedrooms and the privacy of their minds, activated primitive experiences of tantalising closeness and intrusion. There was no formal treatment situation and doctors of the time would turn physician, examine and even massage their patients or give injections, thus confusing what we now see as an important boundary. This "hands on" treatment, including physical contact and home visits, seems to us now to blur a distinction between the medical and the psychoanalytic. It was through such experiences that Freud developed a theory of technique, one that we profit from today.

In her paper on settings for psychotherapy, Temperley (1984) succinctly puts the case for, "very disciplined conventions in the practice of psychotherapy" and it's incompatibility with social relationships where we get "nudged" into enacting familiar yet unconscious object relations. She says, "within and because of the very strict conventions surrounding the therapeutic relationship, primitive, infantile, violent outbursts can occur, which both parties recognise are and are not valid. I am experienced as Margaret Thatcher, or the cleaning lady or the Pope, and we both of us, patient and therapist, know that I am not". It is sometimes only when aspects of the setting alter, that the power of the unconscious connection to the therapist and his setting can be seen; for example, meeting outside the consulting room shocks the patient who finds s/he believes that really you only exist in your consulting room at his/her session times. On one occasion, a patient who had been sitting next to a large plant in the room for some months suddenly appeared to "see" it and enquired whether it was new. Such experiences seem to act as a constant reminder to us that the patients' view of even relatively unchanging decor is heavily influenced by their psychological state and unconscious phantasy. Freud and other analysts realized that the interplay between phantasy and reality created a very complex view of consciousness. He tracked the intrusions of the unconscious into conscious awareness through studying slips of the tongue, the hidden meaning of jokes, dreams and parapraxes. Today, influenced by Kleinian thinking, we tend to work on the assumption that the psychoanalytic therapy setting is immediately imbued with unconscious phantasy, that we do not cause a patient's regression in treatment but facilitate and contain it, as the infantile level of functioning is already present. So what the neurotic part of the personality can see, hear and respond to, is only part of the story. Especially in out-patient work, the functional part of the patient will get them to therapy or to work, but this covers much more infantile feelings, for example, about coming and going, the limits of time, breaks etc. Etchegoyen (1991) quotes an interesting formulation by Bleger who suggests that there is always a psychotic aspect of the transference that takes advantage of the stability of the psycho-therapeutic setting to remain mute, going unnoticed. Only if there is a breach in the setting, such as acting out, would it come to light. I can think of one of my unexpected absences leading to a usually compliant patient insistently complaining, because really they felt that I was under their control, and should never face them with thoughts of my life outside the consulting room. It felt as if I was being lectured by a very haughty employer, revealing a hitherto hidden view of the therapy.

It seems to me that one of the silent factors in treatment is the intense scrutiny of the therapist, where the patient is trying to establish whether he is safe. This experience, picked up through the countertransference, is communicated via projective identification to the therapist and probably utilises acute listening to voice tone, sensitivity to body movements and visual scrutiny at the beginning and end of sessions on both sides. Clearly it is an error then to place too much reliance on what is said, since the anxieties being expressed or hidden at this level are where the testing out of the object and the possibilities of a relationship with the therapist are being explored. So if, for example, it happens that the therapist is unexpectedly absent or misunderstands the patient, he may feel this is justification for the view that people cannot be trusted. Since no therapy can run perfectly and smoothly, these hints are the lifeblood of the work and the route to the unconscious.

So what is the usefulness of aiming to create such a setting? It offers the therapist and the patient an opportunity to see how the latter would usually deal with the frustrations of such firm boundaries. The patient's usual defences against familiar anxieties about separation will be activated by the time limited nature of the session. One illustration of this was provided by a new patient who was very concerned about the parking restrictions operating on the street and ended by asking whether the traffic wardens always came on time to issue tickets if your permitted and paid for time had expired? We assume that a patient's capacity to hold onto the link between himself and his therapist would be based on earlier childhood experiences and phantasies. Once these become observable and potentially analysable, they create the conditions for psychic change. It is fundamental to psychoanalytic thinking that our adulthood coexists with strata of earlier times; Freud was interested in archaeology, so the metaphor is apt. Hence the setting we create should aim to facilitate the process of treatment by providing a good enough containment of the feelings it stirs up, just as a mother contains the feelings of her infant. Bion (1962) described it, expanding on Klein's theorising of infantile mental life.

Briefly, Klein (1957) described a fragmented universe for a baby that is only transiently warm or comforting and easily turns into a world of disturbing feelings of greed, loneliness, hunger and envy, where the anxiety is for his own survival. A primary defence against such anxieties is the expulsion of the state into another who it is hoped can bear it, so projective identification is both defence and communication. If the mother can accept the experience, modify and integrate it, the baby reintrojects a detoxified experience and feels calmer. From this perspective then, it is crucial that negative feelings be tolerated and this applies to both parents and therapists. Arguably more informal work settings or friendships do not allow for such powerful negativity, as it would threaten the equilibrium of social relationships. For Bion the container/contained relationship originates in the baby's relationship to the breast, both concretely and conceptually. The hungry baby who finds the breast, feels loved and comforted as well as nourished and in this sense the anxiety, as well as the hunger, are contained. When the breast is unavailable, it becomes the bad object and the infant responds by feeling persecuted or, the frustration and pain of waiting can promote thinking, a creative response, as the baby struggles to manage without the gratification it wants. The capacity to think, therefore, is dependent on the mind being able to make something of the frustration, using the basic template of the satisfaction experienced when the hungry mouth finds the nipple; the world then shifts from persecutory to satisfying and is populated by good objects. By the time an adult comes for psychotherapy, he will have a long history of such experiences to bring into the transference. The setting provided is imbued with psychoanalytic thinking. It can therefore offer the patient an often new or unusual perspective; for example, that distress can be tolerated, does not drive the therapist/mother away as they maintain the boundaries of the safe setting, nor does it seduce them into inappropriate helpfulness. Such a considered response can also help to understand the patient who may project in the transference parents who are partisan, have favourites, get annoyed or depressed or excited by their child and are unduly swayed by him.

The boundaries also help to contain the therapist and if his behaviour is seen as cruel or indifferent, there is an opportunity to talk about it in the joint knowledge that the therapist will not try to placate the patient and keep things positive and pain-free. This is why offering unexpected extra time, lending books, giving advice or disclosing personal information, are not recommended in psychoanalytic work. If what I have written sounds simple and the counsel of perfectionism, it is only in the interest of outlining the basis of the setting. In many ways it is of course the slips of the tongue or of action, that inevitably occur, that contribute new dimensions to the work and make it creative.

Therapy also depends on that aspect of the setting provided by the therapist; their training, notably their own therapy, will influence their ability to use the countertransference. This can be defined as the particular feelings and experiences evoked, often unconsciously, by this particular patient in this particular therapist in the setting of a session. Sometimes these can be vivid and helpful once they are understood. For example, I noticed with one patient that I seemed to be listening to the noises of a water tank high above the room, and imagined it falling into the room wreaking havoc. I never thought about it otherwise, so I began to try and connect it to the material. It seemed to link his being terrified at home in his own country, waiting for bombs to fall on the house. It became possible to recognise this terror and its motive force in determining how the patient lived. The countertransference is the professional tool of the therapist who tries to observe him or herself as well as the patient and to temper his or her reactions to what is being brought. Sometimes, if the issue is very close to the therapist's own experience, it can touch painful areas or unanalysed parts of himself. Because of this, the therapist will struggle at times to maintain his stance. It is evidence, if such is needed, that the therapist cannot be objective in the sense of being uninvolved in the encounter between him and his patient. In fact there are four dimensions to the situation; two conscious and two unconscious minds. For modern psychoanalysts like Joseph (1975), the mind of the analyst is the central tool of the work. Patients can be very sensitive and accurate about the sensitivities of their therapists and to deny this level of communication would seem to impoverish the contact. Freud, writing about technique in the 1920s, was most concerned about the problems of handling erotic transference and included the countertransference in his observations, when discussing the abstinence required by psychoanalysts. He says,

> If the patient's advances were returned it would be a great triumph for her, but a complete defeat for the treatment. She would have succeeded in what all patients strive for in analysis ... in acting out, in repeating in real life, what she ought to have remembered, to have reproduced as psychical material and to have kept within the sphere of psychical events. In the further course of the love relationship she would bring out all the inhibitions and pathological reactions of her erotic life, without there being any possibility of

correcting them; and the distressing episode would end in remorse
and a great strengthening of her propensity to repression. The love
relationship in fact destroys the patient's susceptibility to influence
from analytic treatment. A combination of the two would be an
impossibility. [Freud, 1915, p. 166]

These are some of the ways in which the therapist's capacities are
integral to the functioning of therapy in its setting.

I have tried to show how certain aspects of the setting are crucial
for the psychotherapeutic process to develop. In doing this, I hope
to have clarified some of the reasons for the insistence on
maintaining constancy in the psychoanalytic setting.

Even the simplest consulting room probably contains a couch,
chairs, pictures and books or plants, so the situation is no more a
blank than is the therapist. However, it is different from other
environments, underlining the fact that the psychoanalytic relationship is unique. These arrangements are based in theory and operate
to enable therapeutic work to proceed.

CHAPTER TWO

"I treat her like a human being": the role of naturalness in a boundaried relationship

Judy Cooper

"In doing psycho-analysis ... I aim at being myself and behaving myself"

Winnicott, 1962, p. 166

On being questioned with admiration as to how he was able to connect so easily with a disturbed and difficult patient, Masud Khan allegedly replied, "It's very simple, I treat her like a human being". Is this important? Should we continually keep in mind that we are human beings first and therapists second? If so, what do we make of an analyst who remains virtually silent throughout an assessment interview, or one who refuses to shake a proffered hand on a first meeting with a patient?

While the other chapters in this book will deal with matters concerning the setting, money, time, separation, endings and so on, this chapter will deal with a rather different ingredient; that of the clinician's mental attitude to his patient. It is not specifically about technique or personality, although these aspects inevitably enter into the equation and affect the choices one makes about how to conduct one's practice. Apart from Roy Schafer's interesting book

"The Analytic Attitude", there is little written directly about this or about naturalness as a component of it. Is there a theory of attitude? Many clinicians would claim a psychoanalytic heritage, but each would have a different way of using it. This chapter attempts to make a contribution to the insufficiently explored, yet difficult subject of the clinician's attitude, tone and style in the therapeutic encounter.

The development of more inhuman stereotyped attitudes in analysts

Let us look at the background to the dehumanized version of psychoanalysis. It should be remembered that Freud himself, Anna Freud and many classical analysts emphasised that above all an analyst should be human. Probably as an attempt to gain scientific status for his work, Freud described analysis as a surgical procedure. It is unfortunate that his early papers on technique (1911–1915), which outlined the principles of analytic anonymity and impersonality, influenced many of the later generations of analysts outside Vienna. Those who had not witnessed Freud's natural clinical style more directly tended to adhere too strictly to the rules of neutrality, unresponsiveness and detachment.

> The result is that the learned model of "orthodox" technique is only a skeleton of the fully human analyst that Freud was personally and assumed others would become. [Couch, 1999]

With the development of "modern" analysis under the impetus of Melanie Klein, came a serious conflict with the classical model of Freudian psychoanalysis. These profound Freud–Klein divergences were outlined in the "Controversial Discussions" of 1943–1944 (King & Steiner, 1991). One of the most far-reaching and intransigent differences between the two schools of thought is that each presupposes an entirely different view of human nature. Kleinians believe that at birth, or very soon after, the baby has intense object relationships intact, and in the first 6 months experiences love, hate, envy, wishes to attack, destroy and dismember, as well as guilt and a wish to repair. In the face of all this, orthodox Kleinians hold that only mutative transference interpretations, based on the here-and-now interactions between patient and analyst, can effect psychic change. In my view, this austere style of analytic exchange frequently leaves a patient feeling persecuted and sterile; but Kleinians consider that their real job is to analyse and the deepest levels can only be reached by remaining as anonymous, impartial and insulated from reality as possible, with a stringent adherence to "correct" technique which is the most effective way to induce regression, and "protect the purity of the transference and the analysis itself" (Couch, 1995).

However, unlike the Kleinians, Freudians have a theory of development, with object relations being built up slowly. Transference interpretations are one aspect of the analytic experience. Equally important are dreams, memories, defences, real-life relationships and reconstruction. For Freudians three levels of the analytic relationship are essential: the transference relationship, the therapeutic alliance and the real relationship. As I will illustrate more fully later, both Freud and Anna Freud had very natural clinical styles which also allowed space for quite separate human relationships with their patients.

Many clinicians (not just Kleinians and not all Kleinians) consider that essentially to be human is to be nontherapeutic (Brenman Pick, 1985). However, others like Lipton (1977) argue that a nonmechanistic, more real experience of the analyst is necessary for a full blown transference to develop:

> ... it is on those valid increments of knowledge about the analyst in current reality that the irrational elements of the transference find a foothold for expansion and elaboration. Without the actuality of the non-technical personal relationship, irrational elements of the transference remain imaginary or intellectual. [p. 271]

In any event it would seem that a well analysed therapist would feel confident and open-minded enough not to have to stick rigidly to the book if a situation calls for a more natural response. In this respect we could learn much from our colleagues practising child psychotherapy; building on disciplined and theoretical foundations, they seem to have a far freer and less precious attitude towards their patients than some of the orthodox analysts in practice today. Even Anne Alvarez (1992), a strict Kleinian, has reached the conclusion that autistic and severely disturbed children come more alive in the context of natural, lively responses from their therapists.

To sum up, there would seem to be two separate schools of thought influencing psychoanalysis as it is practised today. On the one hand there are those who believe that the main force for psychic integration in patients lies in the *mutative transference interpretation*, while others are convinced that it is the *mutative relationship* which holds the most effective key to psychological growth. These polarised attitudes do not help psychoanalysis. There needs to be a move towards the more integrated view that psychoanalytic technique is optimally beneficial within the parameters of a healing relationship.

Definition of naturalness

Overlapping aspects of what I have chosen to call "naturalness" have been discussed by other clinicians under the headings of the real relationship, genuineness, empathy and spontaneity. To my mind, naturalness essentially involves a therapist feeling comfortable about giving an ordinary response rather than a precious, stereotyped, excessively aggressive or withholding one.

The "Oxford Dictionary" defines "natural" as "unaffected, easy-mannered". This does not mean that psychoanalytic psychotherapy should be equivalent to an everyday chat with just another person in the room. This would not be helpful and change would not be possible. The setting is ever important, offering a safe and structured environment, "professional reliability as something that happens easily" (Winnicott, 1954) and "very disciplined conventions in the practice of psychotherapy" (Temperley, 1984) which defy ordinary social relating; for the results in psychotherapy come from a therapist who has a natural, empathic manner but also, paradoxically, from one who allows some distance, anonymity and frustration: there is no necessity to discard one's role. There is a skill in maintaining relative anonymity and at the same time being a person.

> "Natural" style means natural technique within the boundaries of the session. It doesn't mean any kind of acting out. [Couch, 1992, p. 87]

Perhaps being natural merely means not being frightened of being in emotional contact with the patient and his communications (Greenson, 1960).

I consider naturalness to be a necessary and important analytic attitude. There are other attitudes which are not natural and which are more formalised, stilted and uncomfortable. As I have mentioned both Freud and Anna Freud had this quality of naturalness in their dealings with patients (Couch, 1995, 1999). Joan Riviere (1940) describes Freud's professional response to his patients:

> He habitually reacted with simple spontaneous naturalness to whatever he met, (assuming it to be valid in itself). [p. 147]

Confirming this observation, Couch (1999) cites Freud's qualities of genuineness and naturalness which come through his published case histories as well as several reports by patients about their analyses with him. Freud himself never wrote about how he presented himself in a natural human way in the analytic encounter but from all accounts he had a non-rigid analytic style and it would seem that his austere technical recommendations of strict neutrality were laid down to be used by analysts specifically in the domain of free associations and interpretive work where a non judgmental attitude was necessary:

> He expressed concern and warmth towards his patients and quite freely communicated his reactions to their significant life events. He was able to reveal his personal feelings about realistic issues while always maintaining the benign detachment necessary for the analytic process. Unlike the strict conception of analysis as ideally "interpretations only", Freud certainly had many ordinary conversations with his patients, and he considered this a part of an analysis. [p. 142]

Outlining his training analysis with Anna Freud, Arthur Couch commented:

> Anna Freud was so natural in sessions I could hardly see any technique in my sessions with her. But she had very firm boundaries: there was no contact outside one's sessions, and there were no self-revelations. She treated one as an equal collaborator in the analytic process, often asking, "What do you think of that?" or suggesting, "Perhaps we should try that?" [Couch, pers. comm., 1992 in Cooper 1993, pp. 86–87]

In fact, most of Freud's circle of pioneer analysts had a natural, unaffected attitude to their patients. Indeed, Ferenczi took naturalness one step further and experimented with his "active" technique, believing that more involvement on the analyst's part would benefit his patients, although he later relinquished this idea. More typical of many accounts by patients of the early analysts, is Bryher's (1962) description of her analysis with Hanns Sachs:

> I was one of the early group of analysands and it was much less stiff (stuffy I think would be a more correct word) than it is today. [pp. 253–254]

What naturalness includes within the parameters of a boundaried relationship

I think the most basic ingredient of an attitude of naturalness includes conveying the idea that *one is genuinely on the side of the patient*. This, as I remember, was not something I learnt during a course on very disturbed patients which I took as a student. Indeed, some of the analysts teaching us conveyed the impression that they wanted to take a shower after being "contaminated" by the damaged person they had seen. People are larger than theories and cannot always be herded into categories. Patients do not want to be regarded as "cases" or specimens, but as individuals with difficulties which are treated seriously and empathically.

Ella Sharpe (1950) gives a practical guide as to how she would respond in various situations with patients. Everyday dilemmas such as should one or should one not: provide handkerchiefs; lend money for fares; help patients on with coats; prohibit theoretical reading; answer questions; shake hands?

As to the controversial question of touch in psychoanalytic psychotherapy, many mainstream practitioners regard any physical contact as completely outside the realms of the analytic relationship. Indeed, Menninger (1958) claimed that any physical contact constituted, "incompetence or criminal ruthlessness" (p. 48) on the part of the analyst. However, even such a traditional analyst as Edward Glover, in a discussion on whether to shake hands, said that one had to look at the specific needs of the patient and adds,

"When in doubt behave naturally" (1955, pp. 24–25). Sharpe (1950) seems to share a similar approach:

> If we are of simple purpose and without pose, we shall be human and blest with common sense. For anything that occurs while the patient is not lying on the analytical couch, we should be guided by that tact and courtesy we should extend to a formal guest ... and common sense and experience dictate what one does with a formal guest ... If my patient looks for the ceremony of shaking hands, I shake hands. [pp. 30–31]

To her list I could add: how should patient and therapist address each other (particularly in today's informal climate), should one lend books to patients, should one read a book lent by a patient or watch a video offered by one? What about looking at photographs and should one answer the doorbell mid-session? What about supplying water or aspirin if a patient is feeling unwell or allowing someone to use your telephone in an emergency? How should one respond if a patient's loved one dies? Should one give an explanation for sudden alterations or cancellations of sessions? Can one ever accept a gift from a patient? Or give one? Is one allowed to smile when greeting a patient or when saying goodbye? Is it permissible to laugh at a patient's joke, or to ask or answer questions? The queries are endless.

Sharpe is well aware that there is an unconscious dimension to all this which must never be forgotten. Gradually, through interpretation, patients learn the parameters of the frame. We all need gradual disillusionment. Indeed, as Winnicott (1965) claims, the function of the healthy mother is to "traumatize" her baby gradually and too much frustration, particularly at the beginning of therapy, can drive someone mad or discourage him from embarking on analytic treatment. A humiliated and bewildered young man did not return to treatment after the analyst had left his extended hand unmet in two successive sessions. I agree with Sharpe, and although she wrote this in 1930, I do not consider her views to be out-dated. To the extent that analysis is a rigorous procedure looking at transference and unconscious motivation, *patients are also our guests and need to be treated with the same courtesy and welcome as a guest*. This does not mean hospitality. I do not offer a patient food or drink and after a session I see a patient to the door of the consulting room, but not to the front door.

22   DILEMMAS IN THE CONSULTING ROOM

Therapists often feel ashamed and guilty when reporting a natural attitude in sessions, but in fact this could be the more courageous path to tread. Heimann (1978) suggests that, "courage is a prerequisite for a naturally humane way of acting" (editorial by Tonnesmann, p. 311). She was aware that *courage* was needed as her "demand that the analyst be natural contains many traps and dangers" (p. 312). She felt that Freud's goals of helping a patient towards a capacity for pleasure and work:

> ... cannot be achieved if we analysts are unnatural, suppress our own feelings (for example, our counter-transference), or pretend that we are "neutral". In my opinion, there is only a short distance from the neutral analyst to the neuter. [p. 313]

Greenson's (1969) idea of the psychoanalyst as "innovator" could be seen to be in line with this approach, for even very experienced and well-analysed therapists continually meet unexpected situations in their consulting rooms:

> The innovator psychoanalyst is an adventurer, a risk-taker, an explorer. His curiosity leads him to investigate the unknown. This may indicate a freedom from anxiety or a counterphobic attitude. In any event, the anxiety is overridden by the urge to know, to explore. Innovators are not awed by tradition, nor are they lovers of conformity. They are willing to risk being wrong and to expose themselves to the attacks of their colleagues. [p. 509]

At the risk of seeming prescriptive about an attitude which should be essentially open and flexible, naturalness in the therapeutic setting involves providing a safe, nonpersecutory, facilitating environment for patients, so that analytic work can be done. Naturalness in this context can only occur when there is a place and a structure. There has to be some code ensuring mutual deprivation: a "therapeutic barrier" to prevent acting out any sexual or aggressive fantasies. A stance of *"boundaried humanity"* (Couch, pers. comm., 1992 in Cooper, 1993) or *"structured empathy"* (Schafer, 1983) seems the most creative attitude to have as an underlying basis for the analytic process, not as a technical tool (Couch, 1999, p. 147). In fact, with a paranoid patient, the therapist's naturalness could quite easily be seen as seduction or persecutory rigidity and would still remain subject to transference projections.

Lastly, one needs *to know oneself and be fairly comfortable with oneself* in order to be natural in the therapeutic setting. It is necessary to be aware and constantly vigilant of one's feelings. Perhaps Patrick Casement's (1985) idea of an internal supervisor is relevant here. If one trusts oneself one is able to be natural with the confidence of having a secure internalised object which will guard the essential parameters of the analytic process.

Certain countertransference feelings can be expressed and others cannot. All can be used to gain an understanding of the analytic relationship. Providing an analyst has achieved sufficient maturity and has the self-confidence to maintain "an atmosphere of safety" (Schafer, p. 15) in the consulting room, Couch's (1999) "classical" Freudian approach can teach one how to be oneself in the consulting room:

> ... many of the analyst's reactions (feelings and thoughts) are quite ordinary responses to what the patient reports about his inner and outer life. Some of these responses may be useful for an empathic understanding of the patient's character and childhood experiences and thus can become the basis for eventual interpretations ... many of the analyst's reactions are best seen and conveyed in a clinically appropriate form as genuine reactions to important aspects of the patient's life as a fellow human being. These natural interchanges are probably essential for creating an analytic atmosphere of real human engagement in which the full personality of the patient can emerge without constriction and can be fully analyzed. The absence of these natural responses by the analyst, especially when called for by actual tragedies, losses, failures, successes, disappointments, and other significant events in the patient's life, can be the cause of the most serious errors in an analysis—namely, the professionalized creation of an inhuman analytic situation, divorced from real life. [p. 151]

There are those who argue that, for example, the analyst expressing sorrow on hearing that a patient's parent has died, will inhibit the patient from expressing his more aggressive feelings such as triumph and relief. I have not found this to be the case. If there is sufficient trust and acceptance in the analytic relationship, a patient will be free enough to be in touch with a whole range of feelings— both positive and negative. Recently a patient responded to my expression of sympathy on the death of his mother by saying, tearfully, how sad he felt at seeing his mother's dead body and how reluctant he had been to say goodbye and leave the room. He could already feel the growing ache of how much he was missing her. Nevertheless, he was not burdened by the desolation and confusion he had felt after his father's death and went on to express how relieved, liberated and uninhibited he felt and to admit that he was pleased to be able to say this without guilt.

What naturalness does not include within the parameters of a boundaried relationship

Perhaps it is easier to describe what naturalness does not involve rather than what it does. It does not involve *familiarity*, such as in presenting a casual or unprofessional physical appearance or an inappropriate informal setting, for example with family photographs on display. A patient should hopefully feel free enough to say anything without censoring it and know that he is coming for treatment and not for an informal chat.

It does not involve *self-disclosure*. One can have a natural attitude to patients and still remain fairly private and anonymous. One should allow for a healthy curiosity in patients, but they can sometimes ask intrusive questions or make intrusive comments and one can point out their wish to be very personal. Couch (1995), giving a moving description of his training analysis with Anna Freud, repeatedly mentions "the complete naturalness of her clinical approach" (p. 158), but adds "that the usual boundary in sessions was maintained with a velvet glove that conveyed an underlying personal reserve and a benign detachment, but not a technically-required rigid barrier" (p. 159).

Naturalness should not automatically be equated with *spontaneity*. Spontaneity could be construed as unreliability. An instinctual, impulsive response could be quite frightening and damaging to a patient. It is more likely that naturalness will be incorporated into a style of careful, plodding, consistency. An analyst who needs to make an extraordinary or memorable response or interpretation needs to look carefully at his countertransference.

Although it is important for patients to realise that we have all had the experience of psychoanalytic treatment and that every therapist knows what it is like to be a patient, a natural attitude by the clinician does not imply *an equal relationship*. It is essentially unequal, which makes it inherently difficult. Klauber (1981) explains:

> However helpful the experience of analysis may be, its results in the relationship are always infantilizing. This the patient must resent, whether he does so consciously or not ... The counterpart of this is that at present the therapeutic effects of analysis must rely on aspects of the analyst's personality which are able to neutralize the persecutory quality inherent in the formation of transference. It is here that the analyst's ability to listen, not to be dogmatic, and to be spontaneous—which means to be sincere—are all important. [pp. 44–45]

The therapist is there for a specific task which precludes a relationship with his patient involving an equal mutual exchange. He is there to focus, with the patient, on trying to understand the latter's past and present life.

All these points amount to the necessity of maintaining *firm analytic boundaries*. A natural attitude on the part of the therapist in no way gives licence to over-step boundaries. Masud Khan had a natural clinical style which was a great asset in understanding patients, but because he had no boundaries it was the cause of his downfall (Cooper, 1993, pp. 86–87). Likewise with R. D. Laing. A natural attitude and technique is only effective within the parameters of the analytic process. There is no alternative to a consistent, disciplined, safe frame in any therapeutic encounter, but this does not preclude a natural stance on the part of the clinician.

Clinical vignettes

There are many moments when naturalness can emerge from a real situation and the handling of it can be creative or quite destructive. If a patient is not too damaged or paranoid, an initial error by the therapist can often be processed and recovered from. It can be taken on board in terms of the therapist being an ordinary, alive, fallible person:

> Nothing is more discouraging to a patient than inability to recognize his analyst as a human being. No analyst should be only

a talking robot repeating stock phrases and using them as a means
of keeping patients completely at arms length. Even strict Freudian
analysis should remain a fully human affair. [Ruitenbeek, 1973,
p. 196]

I would like to outline situations in which: (a) naturalness was helpful;
(b) the absence of naturalness was harmful; and (c) something one
might regard as natural was unhelpful or needed working through.

Naturalness as helpful

A couple of years into her therapy a patient told me that what had
helped and impressed her most in her first session with me was the
fact that I had said, "How awful for you", on hearing about her life.
Her previous therapist had given more dead-pan responses and she
was surprised that I seemed to show concern for her and took her
seriously.

In a similar way Nini Herman (1985) recounts what a relief it
was when her fourth analyst heard her account of repeated loss and
hardship and responded with the simple, unaffected phrase ... 'So
you have had quite a hard time' (p. 114).

On one memorable occasion the session of an angry but inhibited
patient of mine was intruded upon by a very noisy and chaotic
outburst in another room. There was shouting, arguing and
crying and even the dog was joining in with agitated barking. I
was feeling quite annoyed about this gross intrusion from my
family and was in somewhat of a panic as to my patient's
fantasies and reaction as to what was going on. To my
amazement he responded to this unwarranted impingement by
saying he found it very reassuring to hear a family that was so
involved, caring and communicative, unlike his own, and he felt
certain there was a basis of genuine love which enabled family
members to express their aggression at times. I realised that this
was quite an idealised view, which my patient needed at the time,
but it was helpful for him and we were able to work with it.

I can remember that in my own first analysis, one of the
highlights in three and a half difficult years of orthodox treatment,
was when my analyst laughed at something I said. Despite her

misgivings it was one of the few shared, playful moments we had and I found this human response immensely helpful.

The absence of naturalness as harmful

I have already mentioned the analyst who did not shake the patient's hand with the result that the patient did not return for treatment. The analyst's attitude seems quite bizarre, out of touch with reality. Is it that he fears that symbolically a hand represents a penis? Similarly, what is one to think of the analyst who did not shake his patient's hand at the end of a long analysis? What a jarring way to finish treatment. Not surprisingly the patient felt rejected, nonexistent and had a prolonged depression after this. One might ask why this had not been discussed previously? Had not the patient learnt the analyst's militant style during the long analysis? Even if the analyst felt it was an attempt to manipulate and control and experience a manic triumph on ending, rather than tolerate the sadness of the loss, I think all this would have been secondary to the patient's overriding wish to connect, repair and show gratitude on saying goodbye.

Another example was told to me by a psychoanalytic trainee many years ago. She was furious at the end of one of her sessions and swept past her analyst's bookcase on her way out causing some books to fall to the floor. Immediately, the patient bent to help pick up the books, and the analyst prevented her, saying, "It's time". The patient was so angry that her reparative move had not been acknowledged that she missed her following week of sessions. Even after the event she felt her analyst had made an error and could have made a more natural response such as "I know part of you is sorry. We can talk about it tomorrow". This response would acknowledge the patient's opposing feelings as well as reassure her that the analyst would survive her destructiveness. In short it would have helped her towards the depressive position rather than pushing her towards a more paranoid–schizoid one.

Something one would regard as natural being unhelpful or needing working through

Some time ago I made the grave error of saying, "I can't bear it", after a patient had told me her history of repeated rejection and abuse. This was my spontaneous countertransference response, which was a natural one but was so unconsciously rejecting; it would have been better had it been curbed. It was distinctly unhelpful to the patient. Due to training requirements the patient felt obliged to stay in treatment with me for a couple of years but I never felt we overcame my initial error. My comment only served to exacerbate her tendency towards paranoia and we stayed locked in the predictable repetition of an unremitting negative transference without being able to find a creative way to work it through.

Another example is of a patient who arrived for his first session with me well before his appointment time. After greeting him and showing him to the waiting room, I thought I had commented fairly naturally and matter-of-factly, "You are very early". After many months he was able to tell me how cold and unwelcoming he had found me at that first meeting and how he had consciously had to resort to his ploy of making the events of his mother's untimely death more pitiful, which he felt never failed to move people and soften their attitude towards him. Even 6 years on in his therapy we are still periodically reworking his experience of my initially hurtful reception. Recently he told me he had had serious misgivings about me saying to himself, "Why doesn't she think I'm early because I'm anxious and didn't want to be late? Is this what therapy is going to be like?"

One of my colleagues received a patient 10 minutes after he had heard news of his own mother's death. He had not been able to reach his patient by phone to cancel her session, so on her arrival he apologised that something unexpected had happened and he would not be able to see her that day. He then added that his mother had just died. A long time afterwards, when she had returned to my colleague for a second period of therapy, the patient said "I wish you hadn't told me about your mother having died. I didn't want to know." It was understandable that she did not want to know about other people on her therapist's mind, confirming that he had no space for her, either in his external or internal worlds.

Conclusion

The natural, easy attitude that the majority of early analysts had towards their patients disappeared with the later generation of analysts, who unfortunately adhered to a rigid interpretation of Freud's early papers on technique (1911–1915).

As the status of psychoanalysis has grown, it has become necessary to formalize certain regulations around the practice of it in order to protect it, but that does not mean maintaining a pretentious, rigid, neutral approach which most often succeeds in denying the other person's reality. In fact, the rigidity of the frame which may have been necessary for the birth of the technique, after years and years of clinical work and experience, can surely have reached sufficient maturity to allow more flexibility in following the needs of a patient. Perhaps one would be wise to follow Winnicott's advice, "Needs should be met, wishes should be analysed". In Argentina today it is considered that the better the analyst, the more flexible he is. Many child psychotherapists seem able to retain an easy-mannered, flexible attitude without feeling guilty or threatened about breaking boundaries. Perhaps we can learn something from them.

To have any lasting value, psychoanalysis needs to encompass an alive, human exchange. Fairbairn gradually understood this. Although he, himself, had quite a reserved and detached manner, he became aware that patients come to treatment looking primarily for a relationship. He realised that it was inappropriate to give mechanical interpretations rather than be more human. He learnt this from a patient who interrupted him in the midst of an interpretation and said that he was not interested in what Fairbairn was saying, he was looking for a father (Sutherland, 1989).

In my view, a natural, open, non-doctrinaire style can enhance the, "atmosphere of safety" (Schafer, 1983) within the parameters of the analytic setting. This would seem to be the most effective way of building a creative therapeutic relationship; for without a natural, human connectedness between therapist and patient, pure and perfect technique yielding the most profound analytic interpretations will be sterile, if this is the sole focus of the analytic encounter.

CHAPTER THREE

What identifies, sustains and preoccupies me as a psychoanalytic psychotherapist

Daniel Twomey

Originally this paper was going to be called, "A Day In the Life of a Psychoanalytical Psychotherapist". A day was set aside where my internal preoccupations and responses to patients would be rigorously monitored, observed and noted whilst the external world would be subjected to an equal scrutiny. The experiment lasted all of 20 minutes into the first session of the day. Why? The act of observing and needing to remember material for publishing had a disastrous effect on my work. The freedom to have "evenly suspended attention" (Freud, 1912) was disrupted, my affective responses to what I was being told were distorted and I became preoccupied with getting good material for the paper, worrying about confidentiality and camouflaging the contents. I changed the title to the above and began to think about my first preoccupations which were countertransference and writing about one's work.

The continuing presence of countertransference is well stated by Pick (1985, p. 158): "Constant projecting by the patient into the analyst is the essence of analysis". This is because it guides and formulates our interpretations and alerts us that all is not well and often that things are not what they appear to be.

M started his session joking about his employer's unreliability and slowness in getting things done. I became aware of being irritated by the jokes; this awareness alerted me to M's fury and rage towards his employer and also towards me, his therapist, who was also experienced, but seemingly as unreliable and as slow as his boss. The history of the concept of countertransference has been well documented, from it being experienced as a hindrance to becoming an essential element of psychoanalytic treatment. It is not intended to repeat this history, but rather to discuss my preoccupation with times when the therapist is faced with having feelings elicited in a therapy that are not fully explicable by the concept.

A man was in intensive therapy (4 times weekly) when he experienced a double bereavement within a very short space of time. His mother died after a long illness and his year old son died three months later. The sessions were suffused with intense grief, fury and incomprehension.

These affects were worked on transferentially both in the here-and-now and historically, but I felt that the level of suffering and agony in this patient and the feelings elicited in me could not be contained or fully understood or subsumed within the concept of countertransference feelings. I felt something more than an interpretation was required and a "gesture" was made. I attended the funeral. In making this gesture Fairbairn's 1958 statement "What I understand by the relationship between the patient and the analyst is not just the relationship involved in the transference but the total relationship existing between the patient and the analyst as persons", was extremely confirming.

Just before the first time I had a paper published, I felt extremely anxious and worried. I worried that I might have unwittingly plagiarised others' ideas, misunderstood my material, exposed myself to the ridicule of my colleagues and revealed too much of my own personal internal world. I was surprised to find that these anxieties were still present on writing this paper and in addition I was much more concerned this time with the need to protect the anonymity of my case material. I am aware that it has been suggested that one can ask patients' permission to use their material prior to publication. I find this unacceptable because of the distortions and anxieties it would create and so opted for camouflage instead. I wonder if these concerns and worries prevent many publications ever reaching the light of day?

Since the beginning, analytic practitioners including Freud have been concerned about the length of psychoanalytic treatments and have made attempts to shorten it in order to enable more people to be treated. There is a group of people who often come to psychotherapy with a particular personal story that fills the therapist with a sense of hopelessness and a strong urge to refuse to accept them into treatment. These people have such an intensely troubled and confused inner world that every aspect of their life is affected; they have what could be called "lifestyle defences". These include addictive behaviour patterns, others who stubbornly stay in destructive relationships despite sincere protestations about their genuine unhappiness. Also included in this group are people suffering from severe obsessions and phobic problems who have adapted their total social and personal lives to fit in with their symptoms.

If these people could or would come to intensive therapy (three–five times weekly) one could imagine and hope for an amelioration or change in their internal objects. However, attendance once weekly is often all that is possible. What can one do when one knows that once a week therapy, while it might be palliative, will not alleviate, or as the patient expects, remove the crippling symptoms.

Training as a psychiatric social worker at the Maudesly and Bethlem Royal hospital taught me the value of combining different modalities of treatment for the same patient; this we called Milieu therapy.

> For example, a patient was referred to me for psychotherapy with crippling problems, which were making ordinary life impossible. She was in danger of having to give up work because of her difficulties. Obsessional behaviour and rituals led to her taking 2 hours to get to the session, a journey that in ordinary circumstances would take 20 minutes. When I understood this I thought it to be a good metaphor for what I was thinking, which was, "I can reach this person superficially but in no way can I get to the internal structure of her problems on once a week therapy".

When I thought a good "working alliance" was established, I explained to my patient that in my opinion once a week psychoanalytic psychotherapy on its own would not achieve the results she desired but in combination with another form of therapy, one could be optimistic about the outcome. I suggested referring her to a special unit which could offer her cognitive behavioural therapy, taking care to emphasise that if she wished she could continue working with me (from previous experience I knew the unit concerned would co-operate with such a programme).

She attended her cognitive therapy sessions fortnightly and continued to see me weekly. There was a massive decrease in symptomotology and a concomitant increase in the affect of her sessions with me. The emotions that emerged after the decrease in symptoms were anger, sadness, emptiness, depression and humour. Relationships were examined and without the obsessions, there seemed space to visualise a future. Psychoanalytic psychotherapy and cognitive behaviour therapy worked synergistically to achieve the amelioration of the patient's symptoms and an enrichment and expansion of her emotional life.

This example shows that on certain occasions people can benefit from psychoanalytical insights and practice if therapists are prepared to adapt and work with colleagues having different theoretical orientations. It is important to realise that these different modalities of treatment can take place concurrently. What also emerged very clearly was the defences used to avoid the feelings, which had previously presented as symptoms. The patient needed both modalities of treatment and the therapists, in the best interest of the patient, needed one another.

Most people who decide to enter into psychotherapy come in search of meaning. They usually have their own theory about the cause of their dilemma. "I think it is because of this or that happening to me that I am like this or that today". The need to have meaning and to be able to ascribe a causative source to one's symptoms is perfectly reasonable and understandable; indeed these needs fit in well with early theories of psychoanalysis. Making the unconscious conscious, which was Freud's early formulation for curing neuroses and reconstruction, is still held by many to be an important aspect of treatment.

However my preoccupation is with the defensive uses patients make of reconstruction: for many years I have called this defensive usage the "why" defence. People who use this defence bombard their therapist with the question "why?" as did Edwina, "why can I not stop overeating? Why can't I form meaningful relationships or make friends? Why am I saying this to you?" The obvious interpretation, that her usage of "why" prevented her from engaging in a dialogue with me her therapist, fell on deaf ears. Closeness and intimacy were warded off and the deepening of the therapeutic relationship was avoided.

Paradoxically the continuous asking "why" while giving the impression of a thirst for knowledge, in fact gives the opposite message "I do not want to know how I relate to you, what I am feeling or the deeper meaning of my discourse". The "why" avoids the "what" and forms a resistance against knowing and experiencing what emotions feel like. What is going on between the therapist and the patient? And what effect is each having on the other?

"This therapy is about me and only me
And nothing to do with you or you and me"

was Edwina's response to the interpretation concerning her defensive use of "why".

The danger for the therapist, with such patients, is that the therapist begins to mirror the patients' questioning by prematurely making a reconstructive interpretation or to fit the material into some coherent theoretical model. A student therapist, under the impact of such a patient's demands for reasons, came to his supervisor asking, "what makes a person behave like this in their sessions?"

Continuous interpretation of the avoidance of affect and awareness of the other (the therapist), often relieves the impasse, while on the other hand any move towards pedagogy I have found to be not only useless, but can also increase the resistance.

Throughout our own personal analysis, training and supervision, we have learnt and experienced the power and intensity of the transference relationship. The transference is seen as the cornerstone of a psychoanalytic treatment and the only mutative interpretations are considered to be transference ones (Strachey, 1934). These beliefs would be part of most psychoanalytic psychotherapist's core beliefs, which some patients challenge. These patients refuse to accept or consider any transference interpretations, which are often greeted with ridicule, hostility and an increase in resistance.

"You are always talking about yourself"
"Why are you so sensitive today?"
"There is no need to take everything so personally"
"There are more people in the world besides you"

In such cases, if the therapist still considers the patient can make use of psychoanalytic work, he can choose between continuing to interpret transferentially, hoping the resistance will be overcome, or continuing without transference interpretations, which was the choice I made in treating Mr K.

He continued in intensive treatment (three times weekly) and to my surprise began to make changes both internally and externally. This man is one of a number of such people who come to therapy and require similar adaptations to one's technique. What makes them change?

In trying to understand what was happening and attempting to formulate how change, particularly internal change, came about with this group of patients, it became clear that during their sessions, my phantasy life was very rich and I had many associations, some quite strange, in particular to Mr K's material. I continued to think transferentially.

Unconscious communication between people and in this case, specifically between the analysand and therapist is well known and accepted in the profession. It seems that in Mr K's case my continuous free floating attention to the transference, although silent, communicated itself to him and was internalised. "One only exists if seen by others" (Laing, 1994, p. 70).

A good example of unconscious communication is described by Harold Searles in his paper, "Oedipal Love in the Counter-transference" (1959), where he describes his responses to his 8-year old daughter's, "romantically adoring seductive behaviour", which she had shown towards her father since she was 3 years of age and which enthralled him. He decided that these feelings of admiration communicated to her unconsciously and non-verbally, "could only be nourishing for her developing personality as well as delightful to him" (p. 296).

I have also wondered if I am behaving as a silent witness to these people's unconscious. In other words thinking the unthinkable on their behalf.

> The analyst as a witness, ... is one ... who recognises the emotional import of the patients self-exploration in the immediacy of the moment, yet who stays in attendance without intruding supposed wisdom—at least not verbally. [Poland, 2000]

In thinking about working with this group of people Bion's concept of container and contained and Winnicott's holding and the facilitating environment are also helpful.

Recently I was surprised to find a patient, who belonged to the above group using a transferential model of thinking to explain her thoughts in the session.

> W was talking about her anger towards her daughter who was behaving rudely and aggressively towards her. I pointed out an inconsistency to her. She responded saying "I am not talking to you, I am talking to you as if you were my daughter and I am rehearsing what I am going to say to her when she visits me next week with my grandchildren. I am just letting off steam."

I wondered if this patient was now ready for a more traditional approach and if the previous phase was necessary before a more interpersonal form of relatedness could take place between us that would allow for transferential interpretations to be made.

The last of my current preoccupations that will be dealt with in this paper is the formulation and the usage of theory. I often wonder what kind of an Oedipus complex we would have in psychoanalysis if Freud had been the son of a devout Muslim who practised polygamy rather than the son of a monogamous Jew. This question arose in my mind when I worked intensively with patients brought up as Muslims and others coming from a Confucian background. The two areas of theory that come to mind which are influenced by political and cultural factors, are our theories on homosexuality and hysteria.

Contrast Freud's thoughts on homosexuality (developed in the liberal Vienna of Leher, Malher and Schutt) which were for example:

Homosexual persons are not sick [Freud, 1903];

Homosexuality is assuredly no advantage but it is nothing to be ashamed of, no vice, no degradation. It cannot be classified as an illness: we consider it to be a variation of the sexual function produced by a certain arrest of sexual development [Freud, 1935, p. 786],

with the thoughts of the psychoanalyst Bergler (formulated in the Mcarthyite repressive America, 1956):

though I have no bias, if I were asked what kind of a person the homosexual is I would say homosexuals are essentially disagreeable people, regardless of their pleasant or unpleasant outward manner (exhibiting) a mixture of superciliousness, false aggression and whimpering. Like all psychic masochists, they are subservient when confronted by a stronger person, merciless when in power, unscrupulous about trampling on a weaker person [p. 26]

and again

if a homosexual is a great artist, this is so despite, and not because of his homosexuality. [p. 165]

In 1973 at an International Congress of Psychoanalysis people wondered where all the good hysterics had gone?

Their answers seem to make contributions from the political and social environment crucial. Sexual liberation, the changing status of women and the social acceptance of sexuality were all implicated in the disappearance (and by implication the causes) of hysteria.

These extreme positions—Freud and Bergler—and an awareness of cultural and political influences, have a particular resonance within our minority conscious society and give me a heightened awareness of working with difference in the consulting room. Thinking about hysteria and homosexuality remind me that psychoanalytic theory is not formulated in a vacuum, but is influenced by the political and social environment of the time and often reflects the mores of the prevailing current political beliefs,

> It is extremely difficult to separate a scientific theory from the cultural matrix in which theories are formulated. [Drescher, 1995, p. 240]

It is around theory that different subjects in the title of the paper begin to come together. Theory both preoccupies and sustains me. Rudyard Kipling's famous lines, "If you can keep your head when all about you are losing theirs and blaming it on you", sums up how theory can sustain one during difficult times. It helps me when dealing with patients who produce great quantities of highly varied and colourful material and sometimes pose difficult questions in each session. To avoid being overwhelmed by such material, it is very important for a therapist to hold on to theory and to preserve an analytic stance. Sometimes I find it helpful in understanding the meanings of the patient's material to place the ideas expressed within a topographical model, while at other times I find it more useful to use a structural model. In formulating interpretations I find Anna Freud's statement, "when the analyst begins his work of enlightenment he takes his stand at a point equidistant from the id, ego and the super-ego", (p. 30) sustaining and often preoccupying. Observing the countertransference informing the transference is both continuously thought provoking and a source of nourishment, which also clarifies material and deepens the analytic work.

Talking to and discussing work with like-minded colleagues is helpful and often illuminating:

> I see again how very much closer one comes to all these things if one discusses them rather than trying to swallow them down by reading. [Anna Freud, 1921, p. 111]

Some time ago, in company with a group of colleagues, we formed a supervision group and hired a supervisor to whom we presented our work. The supervisor was changed every two terms. This experience proved to be sustaining and an excellent learning experience combining both peer group and individual supervision.

Recently the world of Information Technology has become an important source of professional nourishment. The taking of on-line courses and becoming a member of the Psychoanalytic Connection in New York has given me access to new ideas and developments in psychoanalysis. Also, it enables me to be part of the international psychoanalytic movement, making friends with colleagues from Europe and America, which supports and enriches me daily in the consulting room.

Reading is an essential part of my sustaining professional diet. Basic Freudian theory underpins my work, while professional journals keep me up to date and aware of contemporary publications. Music, friends, family, involvement in political interests and activity all contribute to professional nourishment and personal fulfilment.

In recent years the question of professional identity has been very much in the minds of psychoanalytic psychotherapists, both organisationally and individually. In the UK people have argued as to who were entitled to call themselves psychoanalysts and what organisation they wanted to represent them, UKCP or BCP? In this paper it is professional individual identity that is being discussed. To help people develop this identity special groups are set up for newly qualified graduates, which suggests that one's identity and being qualified are not synonymous.

To further develop this idea it is worth asking what a therapist does while carrying out the tasks of psychoanalytic therapy. During a session the therapist has to be in a state of free floating attention, freely associating to the patient's material and also looking for an unconscious concomitant in what the analysand is saying. The countertransference has to be monitored and the transference, dreams, defences, enactments and all other material in the session understood and sometimes interpreted whilst maintaining the psychoanalytic frame. I believe that my capacity to carry out the above tasks comes from my own personal analysis and how it has liberated me to empathise and to think about as many facets of the human condition as possible. I am suggesting that at the deepest level professional identity emanates from the experience, internalisation and gratitude for one's personal analysis. This identity depends on feelings of how complete, satisfying and liberating the analysis was felt to be.

Having patients in intensive therapy consolidates this identity. Without such patients the therapist would become like the resting actor who has not been on stage for many years. Colleagues and I often worry about the realistic financial implications of our practices diminishing; however, underlying this worry can be a deeper anxiety of losing our professional identity by not being able to practice what we have been trained to do.

Personal supervision enhances and develops this identity, as does participating in the professional, clinical, scientific and political life of one's own training and professional body.

The work of a psychoanalytic psychotherapist is fulfilling, demanding and often isolating. It is very important for each one of us to be clear about our identity and find our own unique sources of satisfaction and replenishment.

CHAPTER FOUR

The patient's narrative:
the therapist's response

Anne Tyndale

> "Will You, Won't You, Will You, Won't You,
> Will you Join the Dance?"
>
> Lewis Carroll

E very patient comes to his psychotherapist with a story to tell and behind the telling lies a purpose. "The novelist who chooses to tell this story," writes Wayne Booth, a literary critic, "cannot at the same time tell that story; in centering our interest, sympathy or affection on one character, he inevitably excludes from our interest, sympathy or affection some other character. Art imitates life in this respect as in so many others". (Booth, 1991, pp. 78–79). Booth thus points out that, consciously or unconsciously, a narrator wants to persuade a reader to see a character, situation, or life in general, from a certain point of view. Sometimes this is an intentional form of persuasion. The author sets himself apart from the narrator, with whom he may or may not agree, and he knows he is putting forward a perspective which he hopes will enable the reader to step into the shoes of his characters. At other times the author may be unable to stand apart from himself as the rhetorician, he has no capacity to reflect on his emotionally guided self and seeks to draw others into his way of looking at certain situations or life in general. In this paper I shall consider different ways in which patients use narrative and when and to what extent it is helpful for the therapist to succumb to the patient's rhetoric and "join the dance", assuming that the aim of therapy is to effect psychic change.

The patient as author/narrator and therapist as reader/listener

If the reader cannot engage with the author's basic values, he may put down the book; Freud, discussing suitability for psychoanalysis, describes "neuropathic degeneracy" as a "barrier to its effectiveness" (Freud, 1905). For his narrative to make an impact, however, an author sometimes wants to persuade the reader to agree with the beliefs of his second self who may appear as a morally degenerate story teller.

> One of our most common reading experiences is, in fact, the discovery on reflection, that we have allowed ourselves to become a "mock reader" whom we cannot respect, that the beliefs which we were temporarily manipulated into accepting, cannot be defended in the light of day. [Booth, 1991, p. 139]

In the same way the patient, for many different reasons, may want the therapist who is the reader/listener in sessions, to endorse unacceptable beliefs. It is the task of the psychotherapist to help the patient to disengage from himself as a narrator and to become a reflective author who stands back from his story and develops concern for other characters within it, as well as responsibility for himself. The therapist is helpful as a critical reader/listener who can supply the distance from the narrative which the patient himself eventually needs to assume. If from the outset we deem that a patient has no moral sense, however, the therapy cannot begin.

> My patient Mr T spent many sessions recounting amusing and exciting tales of his delinquent activities in adolescence. His tricks and plots gave him a sense of power and of an ability to wreak revenge. Although a part of me was outraged on behalf of his innocent victims, I also heard, underlying the narrative, the

desperation, fury and self-justification of a boy who was watching his family crumble around him and felt that everything to which he had a right was being taken away. I needed to suspend, though not to abandon, my moral judgment, in order that we could both participate in the narrative of his horrible teenage years. He could then feel sufficiently "understood" in preparation for embarking on the longer task of helping him to gain "understanding" (Steiner, 1993, p. 132).

Judgments prematurely intruding upon the patient's narrative may cause us to miss the point. Borderline patients, who want us to reinstate them in a familiar position of being misunderstood, will do all they can to make us judge them. We often unintentionally join in this performance by wishing to be rid of them, but our task is to resist the temptation of acting upon our countertransference feelings by opposing the patient, which at worst may lead to argument and a sense of collapse: a dance of death. In criticizing we wish to alter the narrative and to make it ours. We try to supplement or change, rather than to listen. On one level listening does mean allowing ourselves to be carried along by the patient's narrative: like Booth's "mock reader" to "join the dance". We may fear that such listening will threaten our own identity. It is only when the fury has died down and the patient, still protesting, can say with Laertes, "I forbid my tears; but yet it is our trick; nature her custom holds, Let shame say what it will" ("Hamlet" act 4 scene 7), that we can feel truly in step with our previously borderline patients. Laertes knows there is nothing he can do to bring his sister back to life; he wants to deny his grief and get his revenge. His helplessness feels like humiliation. He is sufficiently in touch with reality, however, to know that he cannot undo what is done and nature leads him towards the slow life-giving process of mourning.

Some patients may want to persuade us temporarily to lose our own critical faculty and to become absorbed in their stories, but we can never do this entirely or we would lose our professional selves and become part of the narrative. In contrast a patient may, for a while, become a narrator without a separate, reflective self who constitutes the author. Booth describes how listening to a narrative with no author decreases emotional distance. He cites the intense feeling of moral isolation in Brighton Rock:

As we travel with the frightened little man, moving aimlessly and without moral support in a world where there is no support for anyone, we come as close to identifying with him as it is possible to come without losing our sense of his aimless, weak, insignificance. With a conventional, omniscient narrator [that is a narrator who is conscious of his reflective, author self] we could only with great difficulty be made to feel personally helpless, personally in want of a champion and avenger. [Booth, 1991, pp. 277–278]

A twice-weekly patient, Mr J, who was bullied and sexually abused as a child, was in a particularly stressful situation at work just before a break in therapy. He came to his session extremely upset. He recounted how, at a small social gathering the previous night, his host had accused him, in front of everyone, of being involved in terrorism some years ago. One by one the other guests turned against him; there was no one on his side. Deeply humiliated and outraged by the injustice of the accusation, Mr J left the party. In the same session, he indignantly recounted a memory of being bullied in the playground, standing up for himself and then being accused of being the bully.

Caught in the grip of this chilling tale, I also felt that Mr J had distorted the events of the previous evening to create a narrative that was not factually true. The next day he told me, with some difficulty, that at times of acute stress he found himself resorting to phantasies of terrorizing people at gun point and he deserved to be punished. We discussed the difference between phantasy and action, but more importantly, Mr J's sense of being unjustly accused of being the bully. In situations of total helplessness, his customary day dreams of winning fights against those who abused him, seemed too implausible to bring comfort. There was no other way to preserve his sense of integrity than to identify with the aggressor in a phantasy scenario where the victim was almost annihilated. At the same time he was, in his mind, re-enacting a scenario in which he was ostracized by everyone. He wanted to find out whether this time his therapist, unlike his mother in the past, would stand up for him. At the end of the second session Mr J was able to question whether the episode at the party had really taken place.

Later I pointed out to this patient how important for the work it had been that he should abandon his competent, reflective self in order to make me engage with him vividly in the situations of childhood which made him fear for his existence. The need to do so was perhaps especially urgent at this time when, up against all sorts of difficulties in his job, he was struggling to believe that I would not forget him during the break. It was vital, however, that he should take responsibility for composing this narrative and that he should understand that it was enough to tell it to me without dangerously staging it in the outside world.

If I had taken Mr J's story literally, I might have made exactly the same comments, which were very few, during the session. However an opportunity for understanding his inner world would have been lost. As Quinodoz reminds us, every narrative has manifest and latent aspects which are constantly interrelating and must both be borne in mind. (Quinodoz, 1964). Although the story was somewhat implausible, my disbelief arose not from an intellectual appraisal, which would probably have intruded upon the affect, but from a countertransference feeling arising from unconscious communication with the patient. Mr J wanted me to dance in his macabre world, but it was also important to him that I supplied (unspeaking) the listener who could distance herself from his narrative and was not caught up in his temporarily psychotic state of mind.

This example shows how the therapist may take the role of a critical listener, able to disengage herself from the emotional drama of the narrative which is told. In this role she is often required to contain feelings which seem unbearable to the patient. The reader of a novel may wish to assume a similar role. Some people may read Henry James' "Turn of the Screw" and enjoy being carried along by the terrors of the governess who believes that her experiences are part of the external world. Others may distance themselves from her narrative and see her fears as self-invented; this perspective would, if she were not a fictional character, give her the chance to claim authorship for her story and to change it.

Defensive use of narrative

Christopher Bollas describes how hysterical patients do not come to therapy for reflection or interpretation, ... "the hysteric will choose the performative over the narrative with narrative inseparable from its informative intentions" (Bollas, 2000, p. 112) The therapist is intended to be an uncritical listener and witness to the story which is itself auto-erotic reverie. The hysteric as narrator does not want an independent listener/reader or theoretician. He does not want to think or to disentangle himself from his mother's mythical view of him, which he presents to the therapist, who is supposed to play a part in the performance. Bollas shows how the patient can use therapy to enhance these defensive reveries and to seduce the therapist, often along with a great variety of other practitioners, to join in with them. Hysterics are, as Freud said, "Dominated by the opposition between reality and fantasy" (Freud, 1901–1905): it is the wish to live in reality that brings them to therapy, but is then heavily resisted.

In a deeply regressed but frustrated state, Miss P, a beautiful 40-year old woman from northern Europe, sought help. Her father had died when she was a baby and she had been brought up by a mentally unstable mother. The patient was an accomplished musician but, beset by numerous physical symptoms, she was unable to carry on her work as a music teacher and was looked after by an old aunt who waited on her hand and foot. Month after month the patient recounted to me how ordinary food poisoned her and how impossible it was for her to stand on her own feet in every sense of the expression. She talked rapidly and continuously, making it difficult for me to think, let alone intervene. Miss P spent her days seeking help from many different kinds of therapists: this was her immutable way of life and there was little sign of any psychological work taking place in, or between, the sessions.

At this stage I could have interpreted Miss P's wish for me, the mother in the transference, to look after her. Indeed we could have spent endless time focused on her desire for me to adopt her, have an affair with her or take her on holiday abroad. Her yearnings and pain were in themselves imbued with erotic pleasure and all she wanted was to draw her therapist into her narrative as a fictional object. A therapist complying with this wish, however, joins the wrong dance, one which becomes interminable, repetitive and uncreative. To interpret this transference is to interpret the mythical narrative which is not the patient's own story but one told to the therapist as the narcissistic mother in the transference, the mother who wants to be the primary focus of her child's life. This mother is a bullying, internal figure from whom the patient imagines his only escape lies in compliantly entering her myth. It is the unraveling of the transference towards this tyrannical parental figure that constitutes the creative dance.

We all know of patients who spend their sessions moaning. The moaning tells us of their dutiful behaviour which discounts what they themselves want to do: they complain that others ignore them and treat them badly. They stack up credits and rejoice in martyrdom. The narrative needs to be interrupted by focusing on any point at which some activity in which the patient has an investment, is reported. This breaks the mood of the transference and encourages free association, which is not just to do with the repressed unconscious, but also with unconscious creativity.

From time to time there were chinks in Miss P's narrative that reminded me of the able woman she was; for instance, she would tell me of enjoying herself with friends in some musical activity which had pleased her. At the same time she usually had to tell me she had tired herself out in order to let me know that such things were bad for her. Nevertheless the patient was giving me an indication of how she might gain satisfaction from real life if she was liberated from the auto-erotic state of regressive phantasy in which she imprisoned herself. Finally this active self which she so envied and despised, (Bollas, 2000, p. 102) gained the upper hand; initially much acting out took place but gradually Miss P was able to find her true desires and resources and to use them for her own benefit.

How much the inner figure of her hating mother was a representation of Miss P's true mother and how much the result of the deeper projections of a greedy, deprived baby, could never be verified, but by analysing the narrative of her extra-transferential relationships and also the transference towards me, Miss P was able to recount how all her life she had felt she must never leave her mother and how unwanted she had felt by an internal father for whom she longed. These insights and a period of working through her conflicts, provided the mutative force which enabled this hysterical patient to abandon the divalent position which Gregorio Kohon describes, the position of being stuck between mother and father unable to choose either and wanting both (Kohon, 1999, p. 18). She finally chose a permanent heterosexual relationship.

Although we often think of psychoanalytic psychotherapy as aiming to turn acting out into reflective narrative in sessions, on some occasions narrative may be used defensively in working through and needs to be removed from mythical thought and transformed into action. Miss P realised this when she said "I have been talking about this (her desire to make love with her boyfriend) for weeks". "Yes", I said, "talking rather than taking action". Miss P said she was "shocked" by what I had said. Later in the session I pointed out that she seemed to want to convey to me that she was far too pure to contemplate sexual intercourse; she was finding it hard to extricate herself from the idea of staying for ever in a presexual state in which her mother was the prime object of her devotion. Miss P found my comment very funny: she was struck by the ludicrousness of the situation. At the end she ruefully added that such purity and faithful commitment to her role as a daughter, was what her mother would have recommended and expected.

In the second half of this 3-year therapy my countertransference feeling towards Miss P changed. When she gradually became able to tell me of achievement and happiness, I found myself enjoying these with her; if she placatingly reverted to declaring that her life had taken a turn for the worse, I would question the validity of her complaint. After a while she did this herself, amazed at her satisfaction in exaggerating small problems and recognising that instead of finding her complaints gratifying, as would a mother who demanded her sole attention, I might find this habit quite annoying. She therefore came to understand that much of her narrative bore no relation to the truth but was manufactured in order to please me, the mother in the transference. On one level she knew this but could not allow her honest, reflective, "author" self to interrupt the narrative.

Wayne Booth (1961) writes of the "unreliable narrator":

> The author may wink and nudge but he may not speak. The reader may sympathise or deplore but he never accepts the narrator as a reliable guide. [p. 300]

As therapy progresses and the healthy ego gains strength, this pattern changes. The reader/therapist and the author, the patient's true self, may combine to challenge the unreliable narrator who eventually steps down and accepts the truth. Miss P's healthy self had allowed me to become for her a new object, an ally who was on the side of progress and separation. She gradually faced the sad facts that she could never be what her mother wanted and equally could never have the mother she wanted: Kohon sees the need to mourn these issues as crucial to the recovery of every hysteric (Kohon, 1999, p. 9). Alongside the mourning, her compulsive need to look after others as well as the underlying resentment, diminished, and the narrative of her life changed.

Different countertransference reactions to the nature of the patient's narrative

It is important to observe countertransference reactions in order to understand the nature of a patient's narrative. Despite Miss P's determination never to embark on the maturational process, her free associations made her an unconscious contributor to the analytic work: a new narrative was brought to light. Between us we understood more about her failed attempts to negotiate the oedipal position both at 3 years old and in adolescence and the reasons for her sinking back into being what she felt her mother wished for: the nonsexual child, single-mindedly devoted to fulfilling her mother's narcissistic needs and determined to believe that the food of adult life would poison her. She was able to form loving connections instead of the very controlling attachments based on need, to which, at first, she saw no alternative.

In contrast to the unwitting alliance which the hysterical patient makes and which enables the therapy to proceed, the borderline patient seeks misalliance, "It is as if his unconscious has refused to engage in the object world" (Bollas, 2000, p. 174). His narrative reflects psychotic thinking which aims to break the link between psyche and reality and thus to eliminate meaning. The discomfort of watching Julian Temple's biographical film of the Sex Pistols, "The Filth and the Fury", provides a convincing experience of being in the presence of borderline phenomena. Although as Temple demonstrates, the Sex Pistols did verbalise the deep outrage experienced by many teenagers of the 1960s, who felt their needs were smothered by smug conventions left over from previous decades, like many of their contemporaries, he misses the point. Despite focusing on a few moments when the group was engaged in reparative action and feeling happy about it, he is, on the whole, caught up in its rhetoric which constitutes a manic defence against a terrifying emptiness. Unlike Henry James in "The Turn of the Screw", Temple is unwilling to offer the reader the option of distancing himself in a reflective way. Instead, he allows himself to be immersed in a false and destructive sense of power thus participating in his subjects' borderline dance of destruction.

In the "Lobster Quadrille" (Lewis Carroll, 1906, pp. 102–103) the Mock Turtle sings a song in which the whiting tries to entice the snail to join his manic dance, "You can really have no notion how delightful it will be, When they take us up and throw us, with the lobsters, out to sea". The snail, perhaps rather a borderline character himself, is clearly afraid of never getting back to reality and rather wisely replies, " 'Too far, too far!' and gave a look askance– Said he thanked the whiting kindly, but he would not join the dance." However, by the time the Mock Turtle sings this song to Alice it is very slowly and sadly. Alice has watched with interest while the Gryphon and Mock Turtle were "jumping about like mad things". She has not joined in but nor, like the snail, has she opted out through fear. She plays a quietly active role as the container of feelings which the dancers want to obliterate. At the end they "sat down again very sadly and quietly and looked at Alice". Unlike Julian Temple who joins in with the Sex Pistols' manic denounce-ment of the real world, Alice does not go along with the mad narrative but becomes the observing listener grounded in reality, which ultimately cannot be avoided.

Dreams as an agent in helping the patient to change from
rhetorical narrator to her true self

Miss P often acted out in sessions by talking in a little baby voice which, after a while, either she or I would observe and comment on. Although time and again aware of what she was doing, she continued this behaviour as if trying to persuade me that she needed caring for like an infant. However, in a series of dreams she found herself looking after a baby she did not particularly want. As the dreams progressed, she took the caring role for granted and finally surprised herself by her competence. Her wish to be looked after, previously maintained through acting out, could only be abandoned when she managed first to demonstrate it in the narrative of her sessions and then, as described by Masud Khan (Khan, 1974) to transform it in her dream world. She now began a period of painful mourning which in turn gave way to making an intimate heterosexual relationship, no longer marred by an inappropriate wish to be protected.

Freud was constantly preoccupied with the relation between trauma and psychological experience. He used the concept of "nachtraglichkeit", deferred action, to show how events become experiences and take traumatic meaning, not so much at the time of the happening but across a period of delay.

> We invariably find that a memory is repressed which has only
> become a trauma by deferred action. The cause of this state of things
> is the retardation of puberty as compared with the rest of the
> individual's development. [Freud, 1886–1889]

Sometimes it is through a dream that trauma, hitherto only experienced, can be turned into narrative. The patient is given a new chance to accept responsibility for using a current event to re-activate feelings about past traumas and through this understanding to gain a different perspective on the present.

Miss D came to me a year after her previous therapist had died unexpectedly. She was an angry woman whose mother had favoured her brother and whose father left when she was three.

She spoke of her therapist's death with grief and rage but although much work was done, it was not until she was able to dream, that she could fully acknowledge how, just as Freud describes, she had combined an external event with unconscious phantasy to create a trauma and then, over time, to let it go.

Quite unusually for this patient, at the beginning of one week, she came to a session having hurt her back; she found it painful to stand unsupported. The next night she had a dream about meeting two men. She wanted to go out with the first one but knew he would not ask her because his wife would be displeased; she went with the second but woke up telling someone that he was the "wrong one". At the end of the week she dreamed of walking round deserted London streets crying, "Just as I did as a teenager", she told me. It was only then that she realised that the anniversary of her previous therapist's death had taken place during this week. She could now see that through hysterical somatisation and dreams she had described, unreflectively, the narratives of her traumatic childhood which she had displaced on to the loss of her therapist, turning it into a catastrophe.

The same patient spoke frequently of feeling there was a "boy within her". One day she came to a session in a state of horrified repulsion. She had dreamed she had a penis. The nature of the dream was such that she felt convinced that it had revealed to her an unconscious delusion. After struggling with her initial disgust at how she had violated her own feminine self, Miss D acknowledged with both interest and dismay how the delusion, which at one time had seemed necessary for her survival, had affected the whole of her life: she saw her personal history in a new light and her present day narrative gradually changed. This is an example of how disavowed reality may be retrieved through free association or dreams. Rather than cluttering the sessions with transference interpretations (these might have been along the lines of her wishing omnipotently to have a "boy within her" in order to please and perhaps also to keep separate from me, the transference mother) it seemed important to allow her to associate freely about her sexual identity. Concentration on the transference relationship would have filled up the analytic space, in this case more usefully left free for the patient's creative associations.

In a very interesting examination of Freud's late paper (1937a), "Constructions in Analysis", Humphrey Morris (Morris, 1993) points out that Freud concluded that it is not only repression of conflict that accounts for gaps in a patient's narrative, but also disavowal of unbearable reality which is part of normal mental life. Disavowal influences both sides of the dialogue between analyst and patient and is intrinsic to the capacity of narrative both to enact and to represent. Freud thought that disavowal could often be revealed in the "kernel of truth" at the centre of hallucination or delusion and he suggests that by free association, it can be uncovered. Transference interpretation which deals with repressed conflicts will not uncover it and indeed may at times be seen as a potential hindrance to reaching the core of a person's psychopathology.

Historical accuracy in a patient's narrative

Donald Spence writes, "Living only for the moment I am not a person at all". (Spence, 1982, p. 458) He sees a person's narrative thread as the core to his identity: it is only if we have a perspective of ourselves in past, present and future that we can feel our lives have meaning. Spence however, gives many reasons to be cautious about accepting that the construction of a patient's narrative through the psychoanalytic process, fits historical truth. He not only follows Freud in regarding a patient's autobiographical account as historically unreliable (Freud, 1901–1905), but also points out how, in the hope of making sense of a patient's life, psychoanalysts may reduce the narrative to a few significant themes, endorse a biographical account as true because it seems to be reinforced by repetition, or regard a narrative account which fits with the transference as compelling when, in fact, the patient may be constructing a narrative in the transference in order to please the analyst. Spence's conclusion is that psychoanalysis cannot be regarded as a science. In fact he seems to imply that whatever story of the patient's life emerges may be pieced together quite haphazardly, both in sessions and in the analyst's reporting of them. The implication is that any attempt to help the patient find a core identity through analysis is subject to distortion; the analyst or therapist may whirl the patient into a narrative of his own choosing and the patient submissively joins his dance.

Spence, however, leaves no room for Auerhahn's concept of "consensual validation".

> The psychoanalytic text is appropriated by the reader and theorist just as much as the literary one is, that is, once created, both their meanings are the object of public determination, subjected to consensual validation. [Auerhahn, 1979, p. 427]

Auerhahn emphasises the importance of an interpretation carrying conviction for both therapist and patient and for those to whom it is reported. The reconstruction of a patient's narrative is not just an arbitrary or random procedure. Reading the psychoanalytic text depends on rules: these are a close following of the text, in which intuition and countertransference reverie play an important part, in conjunction with the use of theory. Just as novels may be seen in a different light by new generations, so, Auerhahn reminds us, is the meaning of the analysand's text teleological: as he faces new life events, new interpretations may be made and his story thus re-written. It is important therefore, that what the analysand gains from analysis is the internalisation of the analytic process and the ability to self-reflect constructively.

If our attempts to help our patients to understand their pasts are in essence inaccurate, how can they facilitate psychic change? Schafer's (1976) view of narrative, based on structuralist and post-structuralist literary theory, discounts the importance of rebuilding a life story. He concentrates on the patient's narrative in the here-and-now with its own inherent meaning and argues that psychoanalytic theory imposes different structures on the narrative so that it is no longer objective or autonomous but used to develop a particular kind of systematic account of human actions. With the telling and re-telling of these stories the analysand becomes co-author and a more reliable narrator. In this view, every statement constitutes an action which takes place in the transference (Schafer, 1976, 1983). Leary (1989) strongly criticises the post-structuralist view that narration itself constitutes experience, making interpretation only valid at the time of telling. She points out that these ideas lead to a re-definition of Freudian psycho-analysis which adheres to the belief that neurotic symptoms have specific referents in the past. She repeats Freud's view that analysands are unreliable narrators but whatever tale the analy-sand tells always bears some relationship to the one he cannot tell. The narrative does not refer to some extra-linguisitic empirical reality, but to the mixture of inner and outer realities which constitute the patient's experience and on which psychic structures are built. It is this combination of inner and outer reality which Quinodoz describes like the ebb and flow of tides, as subject to constant transformation in the dialogue between therapist and patient. (Quinodoz, 1994)

When Mr J associated his story about the previous evening's party with an occasion when he was bullied at school, the origin of the necessity for his phantasies about sadistically holding others to ransom became clearer. It seems to me that this kind of historical reconstruction is essential for solid psychic change. However much Mr J understood that his fears about being accused of armed robbery arose from the projection of his own phantasies and however much he understood that those phantasies were used to be called upon in times of stress and threatened abandonment, a grounded comprehension of their meaning could not be obtained without an understanding of their place in his past history. The playground memory may have been inaccurate or a screen memory but it represented an experience which influenced the subsequent use of an important defence mechanism which in turn was causing him considerable difficulty in present day life.

Victoria Hamilton, in her 1966 study, found that the great majority of analysts paid almost exclusive attention to the here-and-now transference relationship because they tended to regard the past as a collection of intellectual memories which could make no dynamic contribution to the work of the analysis. The compulsion to repeat does take place in present day life and in transference relationships both inside and outside therapy, but as the original conflicts and traumas which motivate it are revealed, insight into their present irrelevance is very important in combining intellect and feeling in the process of working through. We then have to bear the discomfort of being with a patient while he performs, probably again and again, the unsatisfactory dance of the story of his childhood. The music eventually fades, the dancer exhausts himself and the patient adopts the position of an author who is willing to take responsibility for his narrative.

CHAPTER FIVE

I like it when you laugh

Ruth Berkowitz

"If you are there enjoying it all, it is like the sun coming out, for the baby. The mother's pleasure has to be there or else the whole procedure is dead, useless, and mechanical"

Winnicott, DW, 1949,p. 28

I do not intend to consider humour more generally in this paper, nor the issue of the analyst or therapist being humorous. I wish to focus on laughter as a spontaneous response from the therapist. As a newly qualified psychotherapist, I kept a very straight face in spite of sometimes feeling I was going to laugh. Of course, it may at times be unhelpful to laugh, for example with patients who have recently started therapy, or with those who may feel they are being laughed at. However, the patient who said "I like it when you laugh" made me laugh. My response initially to my own laughter was to reproach myself for breaching the rules. When at times I could not help it, I would laugh and then try to understand what this acting out on my part might be, trying to analyse my countertransference response. This understanding and the interpretation of it, was that the patient being amusing and my response of laughter were ways of diverting both of us from more difficult issues. However, when he said, "I like it when you laugh" it made me wonder what he meant. What does it mean to laugh? What, even more strikingly, does it mean to laugh in the analytic setting? What might it mean to one's patient that one laughs? I would like also to consider the difficulties with a spontaneous response like laughter.

These are, firstly, the fears instilled by Freud's writings, that pleasure in the analytic setting will not bring about improvement, and secondly, that there are dangers in being spontaneous in psychoanalytic work. There is the risk of not being containing and of acting out instead, as well as potentially being too revealing of the real personality of the therapist.

What does it mean to laugh?

Laughter according to Freud had, even then, been extensively studied and had been the object of interest of both philosophers and others. He went on to say it remained unexplained and that it would be tempting to say with the sceptics that we must be content to laugh and not try to know why we laugh "since it may be that reflection kills laughter ..." (1905b, p. 147) He does however, give his own explanation: a proscribed idea is introduced by means of an auditory perception, "the cathectic energy used for the inhibition has now suddenly become superfluous, and has been lifted, and is, therefore, now ready to be discharged by laughter" (p. 149). Later he points out that laughter, though not always, is an indication of pleasure (1905b, p. 148). Laughter, he says, is among the highly infectious expressions of psychical states (op. cit. p. 156c).

What does it mean to laugh in the analytic setting?

Coltart (1992) says that she has the distinct impression that in psychoanalysis, laughing is felt to be dangerous. "You hardly ever hear analysts talk about laughing in sessions and you do not see papers written about it either" (p. 11). She quotes Bion (1980) who also wondered, if it is within the rules of psychoanalysis to be able to laugh at ourselves. Is it according to the rules of psychoanalysis that we should be amused and begin to find things funny? Is it permissible to enjoy a psychoanalytic meeting? I suggest that having broken through in this revolutionary matter of being amused in the sacred process of psychoanalysis we might as well continue to see where that more joyous state of mind might take us. [pp. 94–95]

It could be said that if a patient says or does something to amuse us and we laugh, we are either gratifying the patient's need, or acting something out. The question of gratifying needs of patients goes back to Freud who indicates in his writings why in psychoanalysis laughing should be linked with words like "dangerous", "revolutionary". In other works he discusses notions of gratification, of pleasure within the analytic session. One of the responses to this question raised by Coltart and Bion, may be related to Freud's injunction (1915) in which he said,

> I have already let it be understood that analytic technique requires of the physician that he should deny to the patient who is craving for love, the satisfaction she demands. [pp. 164–165]

In certain circumstances, laughing at the patient's amusing behaviour could be seen as offering satisfaction. Freud (1919) in another paper says,

> If owing to the symptoms having been taken apart and lost their value, his suffering becomes mitigated, we must reinstate it elsewhere in the form of some appreciable privation; otherwise we run the danger of never achieving any improvements except quite insignificant and transitory ones [pp. 162–163];

or

> the patient must be left with unfulfilled wishes in abundance. [p. 364]

However, Freud does point out the difficulties of maintaining this stance. It may be that there was some recognition by Freud that total abstinence was not possible, nor helpful. "The deprivation does not extend to everything that the patient desires for perhaps no sick person could tolerate this" (SEXII, 1914b, p. 165) and later "it is therefore just as disastrous for the analysis if the patient's craving for love is gratified as if it is suppressed. The course the analyst must pursue is neither of these; it is one for which there is no model in life" (op. cit. p. 166).

Improvement in Freud's terms has, therefore, been associated with the patient's suffering and the analyst's abstinence. Freud and Ferenczi, as is well known, diverged on the issue of frustration and gratification. Hoffer (1993) points to the "counterpoint between Freud's emphasis on frustration and abstinence and Ferenczi's wish to balance that emphasis with gratification and indulgence" (p. 75). In his paper he discusses the work of Casement who resisted gratifying his patient's wish that he should hold her hand. However, as the author of this paper points out, interestingly, it was Casement's view that without his willingness to consider this, an analytic resolution may not have been possible. In her paper Alvarez (1999) points out how Freud, Winnicott and Bion all emphasise the need to promote learning by frustration, which she questions. Why, asks Alvarez, does suffering take precedence over pleasure? "Pleasure should not be thought inferior to pain in its capacity to disturb, alert and enliven..." (1992, p. 67).

Freud's remark about the highly infectious nature of laughter, although it is a mysterious communication in some ways, could perhaps be thought of in terms of projective identification. One is then in another area of concern and even taboo in psychoanalytic thinking, that of the therapist or analyst acting out, which is one way of understanding laughing at a patient's amusing joke. The importance of containment and of not acting out, or not grossly acting out, has been one of the most notable developments in the analytic encounter. "Thinking about", "reflecting on", are phrases which reveal the need to stay one's hand particularly under pressure. It is this type of pressure which Brenman Pick (1985) considers when she says that the patient may not want an interpretation

> but a response; the sharing of pleasure or of grief. And this may be what the analyst wishes for too. Unless we can properly acknowledge this IN our interpretation, interpretation itself becomes a frozen rejection, or is abandoned, and we feel compelled to act non-interpretively and to be human. [p. 160]

The notion of containment, of the model of the mother in the analytic setting taking in and processing the baby's communications and giving them back *only* after this transformation, is an analytic dictum. However, we do know the importance and value of a partial acting out in the service of understanding the patient's communications. This is described by Sandler (1976) in terms of "role responsiveness" and King (1978) who talks of the analyst's affective response to the patient. They both suggest that this partial acting out is not only essential but inevitable.

The struggle and the difficulty of actually being able to do this without any gross acting out is reflected in the ideas of both Hinshelwood (1999) and Carpy (1989) who suggest that to exclude any acting out may be unhelpful. Talking about the relationship between a mother and child, (as a model for the relationship between therapist and patient) Hinshelwood says, "An infant needs something other than duty from a mother. It needs a mother who can feel the disturbance and to a degree become disturbed herself" (p. 802). Carpy, (1989) goes further and emphasises the importance to the patient of seeing the therapist struggle to contain and not be reactive or act out.

> ... the inevitable partial acting out of the countertransference which allows the patient to see that the analyst is being affected by what is projected, is struggling to tolerate it, and, if the analysis is to be effective, to maintain his analytic stance without grossly acting out. I believe it is through this process that the patient is gradually able to re-introject the previously intolerable aspects of himself that are involved. He is also able to introject the capacity to tolerate them which he has observed in the analyst. [p. 292]

I have tried to point out that something like laughing may be frowned on in the analytic setting, that being human, as Brenman Pick (1985) puts it, is not therapeutic. I do not want in any way to underestimate the importance of the views I have outlined but to suggest that while containment and nonreactivity are vital aspects of the analytic process, they may not represent the whole story.

What does it mean that my patient liked it when I laughed?

Matthew, a middle aged, single man, came to see me because he seemed to have a pattern of abusive relationships. His father had died when he was a small child and he had been told nothing about his father or the circumstances of his death. He was brought up by his single, teenage mother who was tough with herself and with her child There was no job that was too much for her, chopping wood, breaking stones and she operated like a machine in relation to her child. He reports that he was given strict instructions about how to behave and what to do, that his mother spoke in clichés and catch phrases and that any deviations led to severe beatings. There was never any show of affection towards him. But he had a loving grandmother and it was in that relationship that he could faintly see some hope for himself, although the power of this abusive mother was such that he needed not only to be servile towards others but also to be given instructions as to what to do. He felt that any initiative on his part was doomed to failure. When he came to see me for the first time, I was struck by his good looks and his capacity to charm. He came in and immediately took off his shoes and socks and curled his feet under him. What became evident very soon was how disturbed he was. It was as if not only the wood had been chopped and the stones broken, but he too had been treated like this. He talked and talked but my memory is of incoherence, of him sitting in the chair opposite me and my feeling in pieces, not able to follow. "Being all over the place" was all we could make sense of and I see him stretching out his arms to indicate that a bit of him was over here and another bit over there. He wanted to try the couch but kept crawling up and turning around to look at me. Slowly over the years, he was less all over the place, reclaiming bits of himself from imaginary space. I became more and more aware of how he wanted to make me laugh. He had a very funny turn of phrase, would take someone off, or would do a little act, perhaps sing a song. At first, as I said, I gritted my teeth and maintained the analytic stance, remembering a supervisor telling me that by smiling at a patient, he should know what a gift I was giving him. Partly because I am inclined to laugh easily and partly because he became funnier and funnier, I found there were times when I just laughed against my better judgement. This surprised the patient at first, having been used to my impenetrability. I said I thought that he was distracting us both from more painful issues, despair and depression. Too cowed by authority, he agreed with my interpretation but could not help being funny, as I could not help laughing.

Slowly it began to dawn on me that this patient was trying to give me something, that it was his way of expressing his love and doing something to please me. I saw him much more like a small infant not able to walk but sitting in a little chair and making a gesture so that he could have an impact on me and so that the two of us could share a pleasurable experience. It was now he said "I like it when you laugh".

Perhaps we can now return to the point made by Bion (1980)

> I suggest that having broken through in this revolutionary matter of being amused in the sacred process of psychoanalysis we might as well continue to see where that more joyous state of mind might take us. [pp. 94–95]

Being amused in the way I have described could be understood as revealing something of the real me. Greenson (1978) says there are at least two meanings to real, one to do with being realistic and not inappropriate and fantastic, the other more to do with being genuine and authentic, sincere not synthetic. He quotes Anna Freud who said, "somewhere we should have room for the realization that analyst and patient are also two real people, of equal adult status, in a real personal relationship to each other"(1954, p. 372). Klauber (1987) goes so far as to say that it is the "therapeutic aspects of the analyst's personality which counteract the inevitably traumatic effects of developing a transference" (p. 43).

Why should it matter that there is an expression, at times of real feelings on the part of the therapist? Is there anyway always something of a "real" relationship? Symington (1988) quotes Freud's famous statement "it is a very remarkable thing that the Ucs of one human being reacts upon that of another, without passing through the Cs" (1915, p. 194). He goes on to develop this idea further and talks about the X phenomenon, knowledge that is preverbal and it is at this level that the patient knows unconsciously the analyst's internal attitudes. It is Symington's view that in order to separate, the patient needs to gain access to the analyst's core feelings (p. 265). How close is this to Winnicott's notion of the use of an object? (1968)

Stern (1998) talks in this connection about what he calls "now moments" and there is a particular kind of "now moment" which he describes when the patient does something that is difficult to categorise, something that demands a different and a new kind of response with a personal signature that shows the analyst's subjective state with the patient. If this happens they will enter an authentic moment of meeting. [p. 913]

It is this sense of personal signature, something which is unique to that particular relationship, which Stern talks about. How important might this have been to my patient when I laughed? He had experienced his mother as something of a machine and her wish to turn him into an object that could be programmed. Bion, very interestingly, (1978) asks the question, "Why does the presence of a person matter? Why not just have a piece of machinery? If one could get near to being a dispassionate machine which simply reflected back what the patient says, I don't think the patient would get anything out of it at all" (p. 35). Stanton (1990) in his book on Ferenczi describes a situation in which the patient is free associating and there is a jumble of emotional outbursts, emotional and physical pain, laughter when the analyst reacts with what he calls "cool politeness". This according to him would be a repetition of earlier experiences, even traumatic ones. Perhaps that was what I did with my patient while I sat trying to avoid any laughter, and to maintain so called neutrality. Bion again says, "Unfortunately, the whole of our training seems to be at the sacrifice of our animal characteristics or our animal ability" (op. cit. p. 29) and later "About the only thing that seems basic is not so much what we are to *do* but what we are to *be*" (op. cit. p. 31).

Closely related to the notion of the "real" person of the therapist is that of spontaneity. One of the most famous spontaneous acts in psychoanalytic work is that of Coltart shouting at her patient. Laughter is also spontaneous. Could this be beneficial? Baker (1993) considers spontaneity vital. The implication of an absence of spontaneity is that as therapists we always know what we are doing and it may be that we do not, that we are at times responding in a way that surprises ourselves. "It is of the essence of our impossible profession that in a very singular way we do not know what we are doing ..." (Coltart, 1992, p. 2). Similarly, in his Critical Notice (1951) on Marian Milner's book *On not being Able to Paint*, Winnicott points out that "creativity can be destroyed by too great insistence that in action one must know beforehand what one is doing" (p. 329).

What we may also consider is that while I may have in some respects retraumatised my patient and re-enacted the machine-like mother, that somewhere in my laughter was a response to the patient's need, a countertransferential response to his wish for a spontaneous response from me. Hurry (1998) also suggests that some children need to discover or confirm that the object will recognise and respond to them in sound and can take delight in a spontaneous mutual exchange, which she says echoes the early preverbal dialogue between the mother and the infant. Having spoken about the value of spontaneity, it is important to remind ourselves, as Hurry does, that spontaneity must be questioned and scrutinised because of the risk of countertransference acting out. The particular kind of spontaneity which I am discussing here, is not that of Coltart, who shouted at her patient, but one of a more pleasurable kind. I have tried to outline some of the reservations about laughter from the perspective that it could be gratifying, but I would like to consider why a more pleasurable type of exchange between patient and therapist could have therapeutic aspects.

Baker (1993) asks the question as to whether humour has to be gratifying only in the destructive sense. The same could be asked about laughter. What could this mean? Perhaps this returns to Bion's thought about, "where might that more joyous state of mind take us?" In the "Baby as a Going Concern", Winnicott (1949) says that

> What cannot be taken for granted is the mother's pleasure that goes with the clothing and bathing of her own baby. If you are there enjoying it all, it is like the sun coming out for the baby. The mother's pleasure has to be there or else the whole procedure is dead, useless and mechanical. [p. 27]

Alvarez (1999) argues convincingly for the value of addressing the positive transference without being collusive or seductive; that, in the process of recovery, containment and sharing of positive states is equally important as containment and sharing of negative states. The introjection of a good object is something that needs delicate handling according to Alvarez (1999) but "they are the stuff of what Freud called libidinal—and what they and we would also call a loving life" (p. 196).

Reality, spontaneity, aliveness, enjoyment

Baker (1993) writing about humour in psychoanalysis makes several important points:

1. That we convey to our patients that we are more at ease with his suffering than what is pleasurable and enjoyable.
2. Humour, as Freud said, is no mean developmental achievement. It is to do with the mother–infant relationship, with permissiveness, play and creativity. Perhaps the patient's capacity for humour is not simply a defence.
3. That in order to face the painful facts of life, the infant must have enjoyed positive experiences with his mother (quoting Pasquali).
4. Dealing with the analytic situation, Baker suggests that the detached analyst who cannot smile or laugh could traumatise the patient.
5. "... an analyst who ignores a patient's joke has missed what is invariably a communication of great significance". (p. 956)

So those authors who write about the use of humour, about pleasure and enjoyment in psychoanalytic work, are cautious. Baker, (1993) makes the very important point, that while the humour must be spontaneous, it must also be under control so that it can be used in the service of deepening the analysis. Sharing pleasure with a patient is important, but it is a diversion and the analyst must be up to analysing his own response. Alvarez (1999) talks about the importance of the positive but in the interests of balance and seeing the whole picture.

It appears that enjoyment, pleasure, humour and laughter have provoked thought in the minds of many psychoanalysts of differing orientations. In this consideration of the issues related to laughter in the psychoanalytic session, questions are necessarily raised. Is it invariably a diversion? Might it be therapeutic to laugh and when and with which patients? Could the role of the positive, the gratifying, be explored more? Perhaps Freud did not take the monolithic approach which is sometimes attributed to him. After all he said in the Ratman: "In this connection I said a word or two upon the good opinion I had formed of him and this gave him visible pleasure" (SEX, p. 178).

CHAPTER SIX

Money — symbol and reality

Denise Taylor

Money, as we all know, is a concrete reality to be reckoned with. It also has a more individual, relative, but nevertheless essential quality—as Somerset Maugham (1915) put it—"money is like a sixth sense without which you cannot make complete use of the other five." The benefits of sight, hearing and touch are enhanced by the application of money. It is a ready and convenient means of exchange and because of its practical advantages over barter, has replaced the latter since ancient times. In times of want, war, famine or other dislocation, people will return to barter—after all, you cannot eat money. In the last war, a family was fleeing from Poland into Hungary. Exhausted, their young son was crying with hunger and thirst when they came upon a farm and begged to buy a glass of milk. The farmer pointed to the ring on the mother's finger. Words were not needed; this was a universal language. The exchange was made.

The advantage of money, however, is that it is not only a concrete object that can be handled, but that it is also an abstraction, which gives it enormous flexibility. Figures on a cheque are transferred into a bank account from which actual paper money can be drawn from a cash machine. The figures on the paper denote its worth in a particular market. But in the context of worldwide financial markets, the currency of a particular country is traded against that of other countries and the whole operation becomes more and more abstract; nothing more concrete than figures flickering on a screen. The symbols on the screen make almost delicate patterns, but the actual economic consequences are blunt and brutal as was demonstrated by the forced departure of the pound from the European Money Market in 1989. It seems that it is not love, but the circulation of money that makes the world go round.

With money taking such a central position in our lives whether we like it or not, why is it that it has such an ambivalent reputation? On the one hand, it is desired and strived for, a measure of one's success and competence, on the other it is despised as just filthy lucre. The possession of money brings security, power and prestige, but also exposes one to the envy of others. To flaunt one's wealth is considered very bad taste, but to hoard it is even worse. The trouble is that there is no correlation between virtue and wealth; in fact, greed corrupts and the danger is that one subjectively comes to judge one's own worth by one's possessions. Karl Marx spoke of it as the source of alienation. The chimera that wealth can fulfill one's every wish and need inevitably ends in disillusionment with the realisation that, as in the Beatles' song, "money can't buy you love."

While there has been a major shift in society's attitude to sexuality, major taboos remain, mainly as regards money, death and what has lately become known as "political correctness". Money has been called the "modern obscenity", profit is an unacceptable word best avoided and "fat cats" are lampooned in the media. At the same time television quiz shows offering participants the chance to become millionaires break popularity ratings and the national lottery flourishes. In the final decades of the 20th century, the divide between rich and poor has become ever wider in spite of the universally expressed wish for the contrary.

Psychotherapists are not immune to the influence of the prevailing culture; indeed they are more deeply affected than many other professions, because psychotherapy is based on an intimate relationship with one's patient, who is not a "client". Like doctors, psychotherapists come from a tradition of healers, who receive their power from a higher spiritual source. Healing was the prerogative of religious orders. Monks and friars and saintly men and women had the power to cure, or mix powerful potions to make people fall in love or into a deep sleep that simulated death. They were not in the business of amassing riches. From the person seeking healing some sacrifice was required—an arduous journey, long prayers on one's knees, a confession of sins and then, perhaps, you were cured of the evil spirits that caused your despair or you could hang up the crutches beside the holy ikon and walk forth whole and straight again. Riches never could buy absolution and the rich man had very little chance of entering heaven. When in the 14th century indulgences were put up for sale, absolution became devalued and seen as fraudulent. Money and greed had corrupted the church and its teaching and laid it open to Luther's reform and Protestantism. The Puritan ethos, that hard work and clean living would bring its own rewards, fostered the "Protestant Work Ethic" which underpinned the rise to prosperity not only of individuals but also nations.

A central dilemma for psychotherapy is that it is for sale. If happiness cannot be bought, psychotherapy can. On the one hand, as professionally trained practitioners we earn our living by offering our expertise for a fee; on the other hand, we must not act to exploit the sick or ask a patient to pay more than he can afford, although the notion that there is a need to make a sacrifice that hurts if one wants to be healed is still around. Psychologically, what is hard won is highly valued. This sounds fairly straightforward—of course we would not overcharge patients and naturally we deserve to be paid for our labours. But in practice it is not quite as straightforward, or at least not all the time, as we try to reconcile in-depth emotional relationships with our patients at the same time as depending on them to earn a living.

No wonder the parallels of psychotherapy with prostitution have often been drawn. Nevertheless it was quite a shock to me when, as a newly qualified psychotherapist a deeply attached patient said to me, with bitterness, "You are just like a prostitute who hands out her favours for money." To underline what he felt, the patient left the payment for his monthly bill in cash on the writing desk, instead of handing me his cheque in the usual manner. His anger sprang from disillusionment that I was only the "hired help" instead of the devoted mother he never had or the wholly committed lover he had been searching for in vain. To give up the idealised mother figure is hard and to find a substitute is impossible without letting the ideal go and adapting to what is real and within the realm of possibility. The gradual coming to terms with this realisation enabled the patient to embark on the process of finding a good-enough partner. A fundamental difference between the prostitute and the therapist is that the prostitute must split off her feelings while at work, while the therapist depends on keeping in close touch with her feelings in the countertransference, in order to understand and reach her patient.

Psychotherapists have to steer a mid-path between the Scylla and Carybdis of altruism and self-interest. The waters of the unconscious are in constant flux and require careful and sensitive interpretation. The practising psychotherapist has to address two aspects of money. One is the manner in which financial aspects are incorporated into the fundamental structure of the treatment alliance (Greenson, 1964), both at the beginning and throughout the course of the psychotherapy, sometimes referred to as the "technical" aspects. The other is how the personal meaning of money and it's permutations in the patient's material is interpreted. This depends on how at ease the therapist is in his own attitude to money matters and thus in understanding and using his counter-transference in treating his patient.

Psychotherapy trainings largely ignore these issues and one may well get the impression that a psychotherapist only has to grapple with them if they are brought up by the patient. But the analytic process involves a relationship between two personalities interacting in their own subjective ways. Not only will the patient be beset with resistances, defences, unconscious repetitions, projections, idiosyncratic perceptions and all the other failings man is heir to, but psychotherapists are not immune to them either, despite the advantage of having been analysed and trained. This is no guarantee that no blind spots and defensive vulnerabilities remain. The psychotherapist's countertransference can certainly be a valuable tool in understanding the patient. But since Paula Heiman (1950), Margaret Little (1951) and M. Gitelson (1952) pioneered the wider meaning of the concept, the original use of the term seems to have fallen into neglect, namely, a disturbing, distorting, by definition unanalysed aspect of the psychotherapist, which inter-feres with an unclouded view of the patient.

To give a simple example:

A member of a small supervision group for counsellors all of whom had completed their theoretical training, all in individual psychotherapy and hoping to gain full qualification when they had completed the requisite number of clinical hours, surprised the group by announcing that she had intimated to her patient towards the end of the last session that the patient might wish to terminate her therapy before long. It transpired that the patient had begun the session by querying the size of the fee, having discovered that the counsellor was not yet fully qualified. The counsellor resisted the impulse to defend her credentials and responded by saying that the patient felt she was getting second best and therefore should not pay a standard fee. The patient agreed and fell silent. No further discussion on the subject took place. After a silence the patient continued by talking about happenings at work.

The group knew the background of this patient, who felt herself always treated as second best in her family, where her clever and handsome brother took pride of place. He was supported through university and further training and received the lion's share of grandmother's legacy for a deposit on a house. She felt herself to be the ugly duckling, and although she did well in her exams, was not considered university material. Instead, she went into the civil service, where, in due course she rose to a high-ranking position. Logically the patient realized that her potential matched that of her brother, but her subjective self concept was stuck at " 'second best'." Indeed, she had not succeeded in finding a suitable partner.

In the session referred to above the patient had brought up in the therapy what was a core problem or "trauma" in her development which had affected her whole life. The psychotherapist's fee and qualifications provided a ready made setting for the repetition compulsion to assert itself. Berkowitz, in her scholarly article on "The Potential for Trauma in the Transference and Counter-transference" (1999) deals precisely with such a situation, which is common in treatment and leads to stalemate if not addressed. She follows the ideas originated by Balint (1969) through the psycho-analytic literature to the present day. She quotes Baker (1993), who writes about the "dangers of countertransference acting out", which is what happened in the session described above.

The trainee's feelings and reactions to the patient's challenge were anger that the patient should quibble about money when she was earning a good salary and had no dependants, unlike herself. This was followed by painful humiliation and anxiety: she was considered not good enough, not worthy of her hire. She felt she had completely lost the patient's trust, which she saw as irretrievable, so the best rationalised way forward was to plan for ending, which the patient happened to have brought up in the more recent past in the ordinary course of her associations. The counsellor's countertransference acting out constituted a repetition of the trauma and her failure, due to her own unresolved blind spot, to meet the need of the patient. The patient's feelings were acknowledged, but instead of being explored in depth, there was a hiatus and premature foreclosure. We are left with a striking mirroring between therapist and patient; both felt second best or not good enough as well as unjustly exploited.

Freud readily acknowledged that the psychoanalyst earns his livelihood by seeing patients individually for regular sessions over extended periods of time. This was and remains very different from the practice of other medical practitioners. He enjoins potential practitioners not to subscribe to the same "inconsistency, prudish-ness and hypocrisy" with which money matters and sexuality are treated by civilized society but to follow his example, cast off "false shame" and "voluntarily state the price at which he values his time" (Freud, 1913, p. 123). Time is finite; we only have a certain amount of time available in which to earn our living, so time literally equates to money.

But how does the psychotherapist decide what fee to charge? To assume the part of the disinterested philanthropist is unrealistic and leads to the practitioner feeling exploited. Unless there are exceptional circumstances it is also inadvisable to offer treatment free, which is likely to devalue the treatment in the patient's eyes or cause alarm that the therapist is acting out of role. Some patients view the treatment offered by the National Health Service as "free", forgetting that it is their contributions which pay for it. Well-off patients may therefore prefer to "go private" and those who cannot afford that will often use a self-deprecatory attitude as a defence: "I do not want to take up your time", or "I am sure you have more serious cases to deal with."

Practitioners and there are many such, who come to private practice after working in the National Health Service, often find it difficult to adjust to setting a fee, making decisions about the degree of flexibility to be adopted with regard to cancelled and missed sessions, holiday arrangements, loss of earnings, third party payment and other potential complications. Psychotherapy Training Organisations offer no formal guidance. Information about such matters has to be gleaned from private, piecemeal conversations with one's peers in an uncanny resemblance of how sexual knowledge is often acquired in spite of liberalisation. Most psychotherapists beginning in private practice take the example of their own psychoanalyst and supervisor as a starting point; for example in such mundane matters as to how to set out and present one's bill. Some practitioners, in their desire to distance themselves from financial transactions habitually post the monthly bill, or it is left in an envelope on a certain table for the patient to pick up, or the transaction is delegated to a receptionist.

Most practitioners, however, subscribe to the view that it is important to hand the bill personally to the patient and similarly to receive payment, whether by cheque or in cash, as a salutary reminder that psychotherapy is based on a practical monetary contract, which is in fact essential to emphasize and protect the professional relationship between the patient and the psychotherapist. The fee acts as a safeguard and marker to overstepping the boundary into inappropriate intimacy or sexual acting out. Freud wryly remarked that paying a fee also helps the patient eventually to leave analysis. We might add, to exchange infantile regression for the realities of this world. Money acts like the third "other", as does language according to Lacan, to loosen the symbiotic pull in the analytic situation, just as the father does in the original oedipal triangle (Britton, 1989). Holmes (1998) neatly encapsulates the paradox by saying that if we want to find pleasure in working as well as to make a living, if we aim to offer "real therapy rather than retail therapy—money is needed". Eissler (1974), in his comprehensive article on theoretical and technical aspects of the payment of fees, emphasizes that the fee "should create an optimal atmosphere for the patient's recovery at the same time as it gratifies the analyst's narcissistic needs". The analyst gains narcissistic pleasure from his profession, a pleasure derived from being active, or "Funktionslust" as it has been called. However, the psychotherapist has a great responsibility to his patient and needs to subordinate his narcissism to the needs of the patient. He argues that the payment of fees can never be just "matter of fact"; it is part and parcel of the whole treatment situation. When a patient of mine "forgot" to bring her cheque for the second time I suggested that this was not solely because she was predominantly preoccupied with her imminent wedding. Unconsciously she was attempting to deny that ours was "only" a professional relationship. If I were her real mother I would contribute to the cost, unlike the actual one, in spite of her having the funds to do so.

Determining the amount of the fee is a hurdle which many psychotherapists overcome by naming their "standard" fee. This can come across as a "take it or leave it" message and allow the psychotherapist to avoid any further discussion about the fee. Any negotiations tend to centre on the number of sessions per week or such relatively "safe" subjects as the times of sessions. If the patient demurs at the amount of the fee, further discussion and negotiation is necessary. However, it is unusual for the psychotherapist to question the patient's financial state in any detail. Some therapists have adopted a policy of never offering a reduction, but instead to agree to fewer sessions, on the assumption that once the patient has become involved in the therapy, he may want to increase the frequency of sessions and do all he can to afford it; others may be more willing to adjust the fee. The seemingly simple and straightforward solution of offering a "standard" fee, makes it difficult to make allowances for variations in patients' income without arousing feelings in the patient which may never be properly explored but which may pervade the treatment relationship. However, this need not happen if the psychotherapist is alert in taking up and exploring allusions to money matters in the patient's material. Greenson (1973) recounts how he handles the initial contract and gives many examples of how he does not hesitate to explore the patient's associations to expose the underlying feelings.

Psychotherapists who wish to follow a flexible approach might begin by asking what the patient had in mind with regard to a fee. This can open the door to a more in-depth discussion of the patient's finances and give the psychotherapist an idea of how the patient manages his affairs. This has the added advantage that the patient is given the message that such matters can be discussed freely in the therapy, but of course this presupposes that the psychotherapist is completely at ease in conducting such a conversation. It may become apparent that the patient, for example, is "prudish" about money but not about sex, or that he is deeply in debt and quite disorganised in conducting his financial affairs, or obsessively punctilious. All this will probably become apparent in the course of the therapy, but it is better to have some inkling of these matters before one starts, as part of the assessment process. I once sent a young man in his late twenties away to consult a debt counsellor and arranged to meet him for progress reports at intervals. Six months later we started psychotherapy sessions once a week, which he paid for from his earnings at the low end of my scale of fees. It was the beginning of his rehabilitation. We worked for the next few years on his relationship to his father and mother, authority and oedipal problems, inordinate ambition and envy. He had to come to terms with the fact that his talents did not lie in art, a career choice he had made against strong opposition from his parents in a determined effort to ensure his independence and as an act of revenge for what he saw as their valuation of him only as a good brain.

Some patients, in their eagerness for therapy and a desire to appear positive and independent, will exaggerate what they can afford and agree to a fee which is really beyond their means, which is obviously undesirable, as Glover warned specifically (Glover, 1955). If the difficulty is not brought into the open in the therapy, due to the patient's shame and the psychotherapist's inhibitions about broaching money matters, the patient may break off therapy quite abruptly. A patient came to me some years after she had left a previous therapist in this manner, consumed with guilt and shame. Since early childhood she had felt the need to appear the ideal daughter her parents wanted her to be and could never acknowledge any negatives about herself.

She lived a life of make believe and was trapped in her false self persona. As so often happens in such circumstances she amassed sizable debts and was in despair of ever paying these off when we began. It was a tough struggle and took several years of hard work and determination before she emerged, debt free, a new woman, to use her words, into a new life. She had to face her parents with the truth, cut down on her living expenses drastically, take on weekend work and rationalize her debts and their repayment. In due course she changed her job, achieved promotion and acquired new friends.

Other patients act in the opposite direction, giving the picture of a person who hardly has the means for therapy, but is very keen to have it. This may be a realistic picture or it may not and needs exploration. Menninger (1958) warned long ago that analysis will not go well if the patient is paying less than he can reasonably afford.

The little boy fleeing with his parents from Poland, mentioned at the beginning of this chapter, presented a less clear-cut picture. The family eventually found their way to England, where his parents worked very hard to raise themselves out of poverty and establish a new life for the family. Their only son also worked hard at his studies and trying to make friends. He succeeded in acquiring an excellent education and when we met had a satisfying job in a pharmaceutical company. It was a different story as far as social relationships were concerned. He found it difficult to be intimate with men or women and always felt on the outside of things and this is what brought him into therapy. It was as if a shadow had fallen on the sunny, rather mischievous boy who played in the fields and woods near his home in Poland with the lively girl from next door. They were practically the same age and had been inseparable playmates from babyhood until the flight. Her family stayed behind to wait for a visa, but time ran out and none of them escaped the holocaust. His parents, on the other hand, acted in good time. They had money saved and had been able to bribe the officials to obtain the necessary papers.

Tony, as I will call him, was careful with money and kept his affairs in good order. This much became obvious when we negotiated the fee. He brought up the subject himself and said that he had worked out exactly how much he could afford to pay, bearing in mind his commitment to a mortgage, a pension and some savings "for the unexpected event". The fee was at the low end of my scale, but we agreed a fee and he was happy that we should review the fee at the beginning of each year. After all, "one never knew how things would turn out." It is easy to see what place money had in Tony's mind. It spelt security, the means to acquire an education and livelihood and it could literally buy you life. He liked to have as much as possible in liquid assets; "you never could tell, one might need money suddenly."

In the case of Tony there was no traceable disturbance at the infant level of development to account for his attitude to money, which pervaded his attitude to life in general. However, traumas experienced at later stages can have just as serious effects. Tony's security had been profoundly undermined at the height of the oedipal stage by his wartime experiences. His erotic dreams mostly turned into nightmares, as the woman he was about to embrace melted away into a dirty puddle, or turned into something else. Breasts would turn out to be cow-pats and food and drink, however delicious looking, turned out to be made of plaster, just as in the playhouse of his childhood.

Another patient of mine, who grew up with a mentally ill mother, was going through a tough time, both at work, usually the major area of satisfaction in her life and with the man with whom she had hoped to establish a permanent relationship. When this finally foundered, it sent her into a depression where she despaired of ever succeeding. While in this state of mind she suddenly demanded a reduction in the fee she had been paying for a long time, saying she could not afford it in view of her other expenses. I agreed to reduce my fee somewhat, as I could see some slight realistic reasons for it, but more so because I remembered that feeling poor is not the same as being poor. I felt she was in the position described by Winnicott where she needed to take money from the therapist "mother" as a symbolic gesture of her entitlement to loving care, something she was so cruelly deprived of in her childhood. This allowed us yet again to explore the original trauma which, as in mourning, needs to be experienced repeatedly, each time letting go a little in the gradual process of decathecting and coming to terms with it.

In other circumstances a low fee can become a mutually collusive unspoken fantasy. The patient feels, "I am not good enough to pay more" and the therapist feels "I am not a good enough therapist to deserve a higher fee."

Third party payment, usually by an insurance company or a relative, introduces another dimension which may complicate matters. For example, having to give a diagnosis on an insurance form may be disturbing to the patient by attaching a label to his emotional state, which may not lend itself to such a process. Patients may also lack the incentive to involve themselves in the therapy and rest content to coast along for longer than they might otherwise because they are having their money's worth from the insurance company.

Payment by parents can work well. The parents feel they are making up for what went wrong in the upbringing of their child and the patient accepts this gratification while also having the incentive of obligation to work hard in the therapy. However, the therapy can be seriously undermined by the patient using his failure as an act of revenge against the parents. As one young man admitted: "I want them to feel the despair I feel; they have done me irreparable damage and I will not give them the satisfaction of thinking that paying out money can fix it." Relatives for their part can default or become destructively interfering or controlling. A beautiful young woman patient of mine, who lost both parents in a tragic accident when she was a young teenager, was left dependent on a rich uncle who was also the administrator of the parents "trust fund from which he paid the fees for the psychotherapy. But, as soon as the patient was symptom free, which I saw as a premature flight into health, he argued there was no need to continue and the therapy floundered. I suspect that he could not tolerate losing the inordinate control he exercised over his niece, who felt trapped and infantilised. In another case a husband undertook to pay for his wife's psychotherapy. This came to an abrupt end when he left the home and his young family of two children to live with another woman. There was no way my patient could make ends meet on the reduced contributions her husband now made to general household expenses. She managed to increase her part-time job to full time, while I reduced my fee substantially and the number of sessions to one a week.

This raises the subject of loss of earnings in the course of treatment. Again, every case has to be considered individually and one cannot rely on the comfort of having definitive procedures to fall back on. In the example above it seemed right to reduce the fee and cut session numbers. When another patient, a highly qualified mathematician with a horrendous history of parental rejection and exploitation lost her job, we agreed that she would continue her three times weekly sessions she so badly needed and pay me for them when she was in a position to do so. It was therapeutic for her that I trusted and believed in her ability to pay the quite large debt which accumulated. This is indeed what eventually happened, after some bleak times when she went into a deep depression, renegotiating her deprived childhood. I was prepared to take the risk as I felt she had a very good chance of pulling through this crisis.

The treatment of the famous or very wealthy makes special demands on the psychotherapist's countertransference. They are difficult to engage in therapy as they are apt to be suspicious that one values them only because of their assets. It is therefore a mistake to charge them more than one's top fee at the most. They are accustomed to pay well for the best and they have to come to realize that the quality of the service is not correlated to the amount of the fee.

The premature abandonment of psychotherapy of one such well off self-made man in his 50s was due to overwhelming disillusionment and disappointment that, having "made it" had not brought peace, contentment and emotional fulfillment. There were losses to be mourned, like the abortion of their child before he and his wife were married, followed by the postponement of children until "the conditions were right"; but this never quite seemed to come about. Time ran out, his wife became very depressed and had some years of psychotherapy which helped her. She had since developed satisfying interests of her own. For him, his work was his only interest and he was troubled by the problem of succession. He could not bear the thought of it all, his creation, his baby, going to an outsider, or being broken up when he could no longer look after it. In his agitation and acute restlessness he would not give himself time in the therapy and demanded instant results as he had demanded instant gratification from his mother who had always indulged him. He found psychotherapy frustrating, "always jam to-morrow, never to-day". He said he did not have time to go over things that had happened, or were happening here and now, he had to look to the future, and would therefore have to leave psychotherapy. Olsson, in his chapter on "Complexities in the Psychology and Psychotherapy of the Phenomenally Wealthy" (in Krueger, 1986) cites Ernest Becker's Rankian view of money as "immortality power" and Kohut's "grandiose self" as relevant theoretical formulations. Both would certainly apply to the symbolic meaning wealth had for my patient.

The literature on fees in psychotherapy is sparse compared to other topics, but the question of how to handle the financial aspects of missed and cancelled sessions arouses lively discussion. Freud 's position was that he leased a special hour to his patient and this hour had to be paid for, even if the patient did not attend. He observed that it was remarkable how minor indispositions disappeared under this regime—he only rarely found himself in a position where he would feel embarrassed about enjoying free time for which he was receiving payment. If the patient was ill or had to be away for a lengthy period, he would suspend the treatment and resume it when conditions changed, but the patient's particular slot in the day was not reserved. Glover includes a question on missed sessions in his questionnaire on psychotherapy practice which he reported in 1955. A large majority had a standard rule of demanding payment for nonattendance but only half adhered to it (p. 519). He himself came out in favour of a flexible approach.

Whether to charge or not to charge for missed sessions will very much depend on individual circumstances. If the patient just does not turn up, as a patient of mine recently did, because he could not bear to bring a "delicious" telephone conversation with his latest girlfriend to an end, he will be charged. If I know that it is the day of his mother's funeral, he will not be charged. These are extreme examples, but all psychotherapists will have experiences in this regard where they have to use their own judgement. A vivid example of what can sometimes be quite an agonising decision process is given in Haynes and Wiener (1996, pp. 20–22). The therapist not only analyses the patient's reactions to being charged for "legitimately" missed sessions, but also recounts the frank scrutiny of her own feelings and the working through to a satisfactory resolution. Another way of dealing with unavoidable changes is to offer another time in lieu, if that is feasible.

Most psychotherapists are flexible when it comes to a longer term change in the patients' work schedule. As Greenson (1973), for example, points out repeatedly, the analytic situation is artificial enough without the unnecessary addition of unreasonable rigidity. However, some psychotherapists feel strongly that it is essential that the framework or contract is preserved if in-depth work is to be achieved. However, this often leads to adverse reactions in the patient. For example, a paediatric registrar, subject to hospital demands, found that when her rotation changed she could no longer make the time of one of her three weekly analytic sessions. Her analyst responded by acknowledging that this was upsetting for the patient, but said her contract with the analyst also had to be honoured. For 6 months the patient paid the full fee for three sessions and then announced that she was not returning after the imminent summer vacation. She had lost both trust and respect for her analyst.

For Freud, the roots of all meaning are to be found in the body. Money and precious objects therefore symbolically represent the first objects produced by the body, urine and faeces. Folklore, fairy stories and myths endorse Freud's finding. The first reference traced to Freud is in a letter to Fliess in 1897 where he describes his phantasy of himself as a "modern Midas", or Midas in reverse, transforming precious objects into filth. The symbolic equation was further developed in his paper on "Character and Anal Eroticism" (1908), with parsimony, stinginess and obstinacy a particular feature of the anal character. This was followed in 1909 by a paper on folklore, rich in illustrative examples. Ferenczi elaborated on this theme in his paper on "The Ontogenesis of the Interest in Money" (1914) from a developmental perspective, tracing the child's interest in his stools to pleasure in playing with mud, then sand, collecting stones or similar objects, glass marbles and finally coins. His "capitalistic instinct" has a rationale, because it confers real benefits, as well as an anal erotic component.

Abraham expands on the anal character. Faecal presents for mother become gifts of babies. He warns that premature toilet training may lead to premature loss of the infant's sense of power and control and result in huge feelings of inadequacy. He was the first to describe a counterphobic symptom of irrational spending to ward off depression (1923). He also pointed out that anal characters often equate time with money, a connection which may not be lost on psychotherapists! Jones (1950) links the anal character's pleasure in defecation to sexual gratification and refers to habits of postponing evacuation as a means of intensifying this pleasure.

The fact that money is an indelicate topic of conversation is of course because of its unconscious or semi-conscious connections not only with excreta and dirt, but also with sex, as Freud pointed out. Sex in many people's eyes is "dirty", masturbation leads to "pollution" and "dirty old men", who can't keep their base sexual impulses under control are spoken of with disgusted disdain. The old saying, "Where there is muck there is money", owes perhaps more to the fact that wealth was literally rooted in getting one's hands dirty with work on the land or in black satanic mills. The Victorians would look down their noses at someone who was "in trade" and even in America, where attitudes to money are far less ambivalent, "old money" is considered definitely superior to "new". Wealth enabled one to acquire some distance from its source.

Money is unsurpassed in its chameleon-like ability to infiltrate relationships, including therapeutic environments, where it often leads to a long-term, camouflaged existence in the undergrowth of the unconscious which remains undetected. Because its symbolic origins are rooted in excrement and the more primitive elements of sex, we tend to "turn a blind eye" to its pervasiveness, a telling phrase used by Steiner when uncovering the extent of denial at work in Sophocles' tragedy "Oedipus Rex", leading to dire consequences (Steiner 1985, 1993). Money has become sanitised—"Pecunia non olet", "money does not smell", to use Vespasian's phrase (AD 9–79) and we hope, therefore, neutralized, taken for granted, as a given, like our senses. For this to happen psychotherapists need to be able to explore, untangle and come to terms with their own inhibitions and conflicts around money.

CHAPTER SEVEN

Difficulties when a patient presents by proxy

Lou Corner

W hen patients first seek psychoanalytic psychotherapy they bring their own phantasies about what they might expect from the therapist. Whilst some may have knowledge of psychoanalytic ideas which have led them to seek this form of therapy, others may have little or no knowledge. They come because they are in emotional pain or "under stress" and they hope that we might have some solutions to their problems.

The early stage of treatment is crucial, as it forms the basis of the process of therapy but it can also be a difficult one technically. Whilst some patients demonstrate an open curiosity about themselves, others want us to change their external world in the hope that it will then be synonymous with their internal expectations of it. These patients will often find the process we offer in itself a very persecuting one, experiencing us as more sympathetic to their perceived external world. In trying to offer a facilitating environment we can be tempted into colluding with them in seeing themselves only as victims. In this way, I would suggest, we too run the risk of becoming the "victims" of their circumstance, rather than enabling them to explore their own contribution to their current predicament.

Our initial work as therapists is to bring about a shift in the patient's thinking, to assist them begin the process of gaining an understanding of their own inner psychic functioning. Whilst projection as a defence mechanism occurs throughout therapy from time to time for any patient, some will use excessive projective identification and as a result lose themselves in the identity of others. This mechanism shows clearly in the early stages and it is the issue of technique that I wish to address here. I refer specifically to those patients who continuously bring projected material to the sessions, focusing upon a partner or others in their life. They are unable to function in their own right and as a result their capacity for thinking with us in the consulting room is lost, making it difficult for us in the transference.

For such patients, having split off the part of themselves they cannot tolerate and having projected it into the object, they then feel persecuted by this object. This in itself creates a dependency upon the object and this defence mechanism of splitting and projection is extended to others around them. It is then a prominent person in their lives whom they initially present to us as "the problem". They hope that the insights gained in therapy belong to and will change the external object, thus enabling them to deny any responsibility for the situation. Alternatively patients may initially present themselves as the bad object, having split off the good aspects of themselves, hoping we will change them for the benefit of these idealized others. They experience themselves as depleted of any sense of self worth. During the course of therapy this is revealed as a defence against their rage with the idealized object whom they now wish us to change.

One category of patients in whom this mechanism can be observed frequently, from my experience, is married women who present their husbands rather than themselves in the first instance. Although they express great unhappiness within their marriage they give financial dependence as the reason why they cannot leave their spouses. Yet apparently in contradiction, such patients seem to fear that if they are to make changes in themselves, separation from their husbands will be the inevitable conclusion. Consequently they are often resistant to the treatment and spouses, too, are sometimes presented as hostile to the therapy. We might speculate that they also fear a change in their wives. That one or both partners now fears that therapy will make divorce the inevitable outcome could, in some ways, be an indication that they understand a "truth". Therapy, if it goes well, will lead to a separation, although not necessarily one of such a concrete nature. For the patient this also leads to a further painful dilemma as she will inevitably become dependent upon the therapist at a very early stage, leading to a conflict within her in terms of who she will give up, husband or therapist. This is as yet an unconscious process and therefore unavailable to her.

Etchegoyen (1991) when considering some of the indications and contra-indications for analysis, suggests that if the patient is in a family hostile to analysis, this should be a consideration which is further compounded if the patient is a wife economically dependent on her husband.

> In our culture, a husband who maintains his family and wants to be
> analysed, in opposition to his wife's wishes, will be an easier patient
> than a woman economically dependent on her husband, consider-
> ing as equal for both the extent of the projection of the resistance on
> to the spouse. These factors, although they do not touch the essence
> of the analysis, should be weighed at the time of indication. [p. 26]

It is interesting to consider this in our culture now when women form a large percentage of the workplace. In my experience when faced with such patients, it is not usually those with young children who opt to stay at home, but those who could now earn if they chose to do so, but whose resistance to internal or external change does not allow them to contemplate such an action. It should also be noted that in such patients, although the hostility within the husband may well be present, in private practice the fees materialize despite it. Whilst I would not wish to dismiss the financial problems that divorce inevitably incurs, I have come to think about the issue more as one of the inner impoverishment such patients fear if they leave their husbands and as a result, the projected part of themselves he now contains. As they begin to take back such projections and take responsibility for themselves, the issue of financial dependence recedes.

Whilst the subject of dependency can be thought of in a number of ways, I wish to focus here upon the dependency created by the use of excessive projective identification. In the illustrations I shall present, early environmental failure is prominent in each case. Due to the experience of loss as a result of withdrawal by the original object, the patients never experienced a gradual separation process. They then sought this early attachment in their adult relationships. Whilst these examples of withdrawal are more extreme, there are aspects which can be identified in many patients where dependency is an issue. Although not all female patients who are dependent upon their husbands will present the mechanisms that my case material will demonstrate, nevertheless I have been struck by how often it occurs. However, I have included an illustration of a male patient, as this scenario is certainly not exclusive to women.

When working with such patients, it is inevitable that this defence mechanism of splitting and projection will present itself within the consulting room from the beginning, evoking counter-transference responses which can tempt the therapist either to try to replace the original object, or, by being rejecting, repeat the patient's experience. The intensity of such defence mechanisms can be considerable and how one deals with it is crucial in terms of whether we merely create a supportive environment, which may assist the patient to function a little more effectively, or whether we bring about any longer lasting psychic change.

I want to first consider the mechanism of projective identification both as a healthy process and as a resistance to development. Klein (1946) described the process of splitting off part of the self and projecting it into an object as of vital importance for normal development. In describing the process of projection and introjection (1946, 1952, 1955) she states that this mechanism operates from the start of the infant's life and through a complex interaction between the mother and baby, the infant builds up its internal world which in turn shapes its perception of external reality. She describes how the infant introjects its objects, (initially in the form of part object/breast) and through the interaction between these now internalized objects and the infant's own ego, fragile though it might be at this time, the infant will either experience the world as mainly hostile and dangerous or loving and good. Klein sees a distinction between these introjections as either a negative or positive experience, but both are part of a continuing process. However, she considers that the first anxiety for the infant is persecutory, arising from the experience of birth and that this initial anxiety gives rise to a feeling within the infant that what he introjects appears to be hostile. When the infant begins to feel gratified he then experiences a positive introjection and thus his object (breast) will be experienced as loving and good. Whilst this process is one that is part of normal development and indeed is essential to the gradual gaining of individual identity, Klein (1955) goes on to state that:

> It is of course profoundly influenced by his good and bad experiences from external sources. [p. 310]

In other words, whilst the infant's anxieties of a persecutory or depressive nature will influence how they integrate these introjections and what they can and cannot tolerate and therefore project, the attitude of the mother and her capacity to tolerate the projections of her infant is also vital.

Klein (1955) asserts that when the individual manages to split off part of himself and identifies the projection in the object into which this split off part is projected, this aspect of himself is now lost, leading to a feeling of depletion and inadequacy.

Bion (1959) also examines the consequences of any disturbance in this process and sees the origins as twofold. The first is the patient's own predisposition to excessively destructive feelings (for example, hatred or envy) and the second being when the environment denies the infant the use of projective identification. He sees that projective identification enables the infant to "investigate his own feelings in a personality powerful enough to contain them" (p. 106). If either the infant's own feelings of destruction or the mother's incapacity to act as the repository for these feelings hinder the process then this will prevent the development of curiosity on the part of the infant, without which the infant is unable to learn.

In normal development, the infant evacuates the part of himself that he finds intolerable, into the breast. This enables him to perceive that he then retrieves this part of himself in an altered and more manageable form. If the destructive aspect of himself has to destroy any positive introjections or if his object is unavailable to him as a transformer, then the retrieved part of himself may either become more persecutory or be experienced as having a deadening quality.

Ogden (1994) considers that there are two aspects of projective identification: the unconscious phantasy of evacuating part of oneself into another person and the interpersonal quality of projective identification, where the recipient (mother/therapist) negates herself as a separate subject, thus making psychological room to be taken over by the object.

Malin and Grotstein (1966) also emphasize the combined effort of both the infant and the infant's environment as being a necessary partnership for this mechanism to either develop along healthy lines or to become excessive in the case of environmental failure. They go on to say that the essence of the therapeutic process is through modification of internal object relationships within the ego, which is brought about by correct interpretations of the projective identification. This becomes evident in the illustrations that now follow.

In this case material I am only presenting the initial stages of treatment. As they have become fixated at this early phase, it is my contention that the very first contact with the therapist in itself provides an illustration of how such patients experienced their infancy.

Mrs D

Mrs D, a patient in her late 30s was referred to me diagnosed with severe depression. At times in her life she had been totally unable to function. There had been a number of suicide attempts and she presented to her doctor with many somatic symptoms. She had previously received various forms of help and had been admitted to hospital on two occasions. All therapists, she explained, had failed to understand her. She had two daughters but at times could not look after them and her husband was then called upon to do so whilst she remained in bed.

Mrs D described her husband as very controlling and at times frightening. He did not like to socialize and she had to have the house just right for him with his supper on the table when he came in from work. However, she also made it quite clear to me that she needed him and could not survive alone. She did not earn an income and considered that she was incapable of sustaining work.

Mrs D told me that she was adopted when she was 6 weeks old. It was quickly apparent that she preserved her birth mother as a good (idealized) object whom, she was sure, was a victim of circumstance. On the other hand, she described her adoptive mother as cold, distant and bad. Mrs D did not feel loved by her adoptive mother whom she felt regretted adopting her. She had been closer to her adoptive father but he had died when she was 10 years old.

In trying to arrange our initial session, Mrs D had had great difficulty in being able to accept any of the times offered. She told me that she thought I ought to fit the timing of our sessions with the train timetable. She explained that *I* lived some distance away from *her*. Having finally decided to accept a session which wasted her time the least, she arrived and informed me that the train timetable was now to change and could we please keep this in mind for any future appointments.

Mrs D then went on to tell me her history. Her previous treatment had ensured that she knew how to present this to me. I initially began to think about these two mothers and considered the transference. Was I to be the idealized mother or the cold, distant, critical adoptive mother? I thought about the difficulty in arranging the session time and interpreted to her that she thought that I was distant, and that, like her past therapists, I would also be unable to help her.

However, as she began to tell me about her husband, his need to control and her need to get the house right for him, I realized that she had been successfully presenting as him whilst I was left with the experience of being her. I could not get it right for her and I should have her sessions ready for her on the table when she arrives at her therapeutic home. I interpreted that she wanted me to know how it felt to be her, on the receiving end of this husband and her attempt to control me in determining our session times was a way of letting me know how this feels. This brought about a response quite different from the one in which I made my initial transference interpretation, which she had ignored. Now she stopped and remained quite silent. Then she said: "I can do some shopping if I get here too early for a session."

In thinking about this session and her response to my interventions, I came to understand how the transference interpretation of me as yet another useless therapist/adoptive mother was
probably correct, but not at all helpful. The splitting process for
this patient had been aided by the fact that she had two mothers
and had successfully projected into them the good and bad parts
of herself, leaving herself totally depleted. As the treatment went
on, it became clearer to us both that her depression enabled her
to regress to becoming the helpless infant who would be looked
after, either by her husband or a hospital.

My interpretation in regard to the projective identification,
however, had resonated within her, although at this stage she
was unable to think about it with me, but instead changed her
behaviour. Of course, she did not actually become her husband
but was able to demonstrate that part of her that she so
successfully projected into him. But she then had to project the
helpless part of herself into me, as she was unable to contain
both the aggressive and the helpless parts of herself, at the same
time. I could have interpreted the projection by simply drawing
attention to the aggressive part of herself but in listening to my
countertransference response to her within this session, I found
that rather than feeling irritated by her need to control me, I
experienced an infant whose own irritation I could tolerate.

It should be said that this process went on for a considerable
time before any real understanding and corresponding change
occurred for this patient. Indeed, after 10 months she suddenly
took a flight into health, deciding that she would leave the
therapy, grateful that she was "so transformed", although
clearly little had changed for her. This left me somewhat
puzzled and no amount of understanding on my part of the
idealized transference seemed to alleviate my feeling that I had
failed her, that I had not been a good enough therapist for her
despite all her statements to the contrary. Four months later she
returned to therapy and I found myself asking a direct question.
When was she adopted? "I was 10 months old" she replied, "6
weeks when I was fostered but 10 months when the adoption
took place". Thus she left me, letting me know how it felt to be

abandoned by splitting this part of herself and projecting it into me.

From this point on we were able to work much more with an understanding of the splitting process. It was as if Mrs D had to act out this initial trauma of separation before she could develop a more healthy attachment to me, in which she could begin to reintegrate the parts of herself she had projected and explore her inner negative phantasies.

Mr Y

Mr Y presented to me for treatment aged 46. He lived at home with his father, having only had one brief attempt to leave home, aged 18, when he went to university. However, he dropped out at the end of his first year. Mr Y's mother left the family home when he was 8 years old, leaving him and his brother with his father. Mr Y occasionally saw his mother but had no interest in doing so. He experienced her as withdrawn and emotionally detached, a shadowy figure. He thought she had been very depressed in his early years and that she had a drink problem.

Mr Y's father was older than his wife by some years and when Mr Y returned home from university, his father had taken retirement. He then looked after Mr Y by carrying out all the household tasks and would have his "tea" ready for him each day as he returned from work. Mr Y would constantly complain in the early stages of the therapy that his father produced a limited range of cooking and that he hated having to sit with him over his "tea", as he found his conversation boring. He told me he did not like his father much and felt he had made nothing of himself.

Mr Y's relationships with women had never lasted. At work he had good relationships with his colleagues, but he saw authority figures as persecuting and he would constantly make derisory comments about them along the lines that they had conformed to society norms with mortgages, 2.4 children and package holidays.

Mr Y was employed in fairly menial work which was below his capabilities. His boss had frequently tried to encourage him to take further training or to go for internal promotion but Mr Y had declined. He was very bored with the work but could not make up his mind what he wanted to do as an alternative. It was his low income that kept him from leaving home, he explained.

At one stage in our first session Mr Y told me that he had difficulty in relating to anyone smaller than himself. I noted that the patient was extremely tall; he was telling me he had difficulties with everyone, including me.

When patients ring me to make their first appointment I always give them some instructions about how they will find my front door, due to its location. A lot can be gleaned from how they receive this information and I can usually predict those who will get lost. Mr Y was such a patient. He arrived late to this initial session because he had both got lost and had been into my neighbour's house. He then managed to get into my back garden, walking past my front door to do so and I eventually had to go and fetch him. The theme throughout this session was that he felt he was not good enough, that he sought perfection. Alongside this he constantly referred to the fact that other people thought he should do this or that.

Throughout the session the patient wandered from one thing to another, apologized for going off the subject but continued to drift. I found myself at times confused about his history as a result, but sensed that this confusion was more important to understand than actually getting an accurate history.

At one point during the session Mr Y began to make an interpretation about why he felt he was depressed but then stopped and said apologetically: "Sorry, that is your job." I picked this up in terms of his not valuing his own thoughts and ideas and thinking that I would do the same. He looked very surprised as if I had read his mind and agreed. He continued to wander through his life and moved around, constantly conveying a sense of nervousness. I felt that he wanted to get it right for me. However, when I later began an interpretation to this effect he interrupted me by saying, "you do not need to tell me that, I know all that already".

At the end of the session he began talking about how difficult he found it to finish things. He clearly found it difficult to end this session and his departure was as problematic as his arrival.

In thinking about this session I gained an impression of someone who had not yet any sense of himself, that he was all over the place, fragmented, and I reflected to myself the way he had arrived for this session. Finding a therapeutic home was problematic, he was lost and I began to consider what this meant in terms of a re-creation of his early infant relationship with his mother.

Throughout the early stages of therapy the patient lay on the couch complaining about the outside world. The women were all so critical and the men controlling, making him do things he did not want to do. He would go into lengthy explanations about attendants in car parks making him park his car in the spaces provided, or his boss who wanted him in on time in the morning when he could see no reason why. He expressed surprise at any transference interpretations I made, in that I was clearly reading his mind. I found myself, as I had in the first session, in "two minds" about my response to this. It could be that I was indeed very much in touch with the patient and this in itself brought about relief of the kind that occurs when we connect with something inside the patient, enabling them to begin thinking about the issue. However, this did not appear to be the case for Mr Y. I had the feeling that whilst it would be tempting to congratulate myself on being in touch, he was actually keeping me at a distance. I found myself more and more feeling like the father who fed him food he did not want, or the boss who was trying to encourage him to be curious in order to get promotion. His responses to any interpretations to this effect left me feeling useless and inadequate. He was very passive in the way he dealt with aspects of his life, shutting himself off in the evenings rather than participating in any social activity, walking away from any interaction which might engage him in conflict. So, too, on the couch he lay complaining with little attempt to reflect on himself, his external situation or his relationship with me in the session. I found my own mind wandering and also often became very sleepy in the sessions.

I came to understand that projective identification could be experienced on two levels. Mr Y projected all his aggressive aspects into other people and then felt totally controlled and persecuted by them. He left himself empty of any potent energy and was unable to function other than as a recipient of other people's projections. In his sessions with me, I had initially interpreted that he also experienced me as critical and control-ling, like the others in his life. However, I gradually came to realize that on the contrary, he had successfully projected into me his own unconscious feeling of being the inadequate, passive infant who could not please his mother, could not bring her alive. I began to see the infant before me who had given up on the attempt to get his mother to contain his projections and hand them back in a more manageable form. He had "cut off" and in this way he mirrored his experience of his unavailable mother. It was only when I was able to help him see that he was making me into himself as his only way of communicating to me his real despair, that we began to bring the relationship into the transference. It is true that the transference interpretations I had been making were probably valid, but they had no resonance for this patient who was still trying to attach himself to a primary maternal object before he could gain a sense of separate identity.

Discussion

Greenson (1967) states:

> neurotic transference phenomena indicate that the patient has a stable self representation which is sharply differentiated from his object representations. [p. 174]

The patients I present above were still operating in a pre-oedipal stage, seeking a good object to replace the original lost object. The failure of the mother to act in this capacity had led to a splitting process so that the unacceptable parts of the patient were then projected into any subsequent relationships. They then bring a depleted self to the consulting room.

Freud (1917) drew the comparisons between mourning the lost object and melancholia and stated that:

> In some people the same influences produce melancholia instead of mourning and we consequently suspect them of a pathological disposition. [p. 243]

He links melancholia to an object-loss withdrawn from consciousness so that the patient knows *whom* he has lost but not *what* he has lost. He makes the distinction between mourning, where the loss is conscious and leaves the external world empty, and melancholia where the loss is within the ego itself leaving the patient feeling empty, worthless, incapable of achievement. As can be seen from Mrs D and Mr Y, this is then projected into the external world as a means of defence against such feelings, although this in itself now leaves them empty and thus they suffer a further, unidentified loss. Freud sees that in melancholic patients, the libido is withdrawn from the object choice into the ego. This in turn establishes identification with the lost object within the ego. He goes on to think about the narcissistic identification with the object which Mrs D and Mr Y demonstrated clearly at different stages in their treatment.

Meltzer (1967) describes massive projective identification as the best defence against separation anxiety. The patients I describe continued to use this means of defence as opposed to making effective use of other objects available to them as a replacement for the original object. Whilst I would not wish to deny the level of the narcissistic wound that was experienced by each patient, due to environmental failure, I would also agree with Bion that it can never be environmental failure alone. As Freud states (quoted above) there is a predisposition within these patients to resort to melancholia rather than a displacement onto another person. What I try to demonstrate in the case illustrations is how this early experience is recreated within the consulting room in the very first session. A patient who is functioning at an oedipal level will not display the pre-oedipal experience with such clarity.

Grinberg (1962) used the term "projective counter-identification" to describe the therapist's response to the patient's excessive use of projective identification. He talks about this aspect of countertransference (which he distinguishes from other forms of countertransference) as occurring when a patient's projective identification mechanism becomes too active, due either to an exaggerated intensity of its emotional charges or to the violent way in which it was introjected from its object during childhood. He states that:

> In some cases, projective counter-identification may become a positive element in the analysis, since it clarifies to the analyst some of the patient's contents and attitudes determined by projective identification, and makes possible certain interpretations, whose emergence could not be otherwise explained. [p. 205]

In the cases I present above it was only in being able to experience myself "as if" I had now become the patient that I could begin to understand what it felt like to be this patient. I am suggesting too that as this early experience of loss occurred when the patient was as yet without words to describe his or her feelings, he or she found it hard to communicate other than by means of projective identification. The words used in making the transference interpretations had no meaning as yet because they belong to a later stage of development.

Summary

I have tried to think about the technique we might need to employ when the patient coming for psychoanalytic psychotherapy presents through other people rather than themselves. This type of patient will complain constantly about the outside world but show little curiosity about it or themselves. They feel stuck in their own lives and consider this to be the fault of those around them. However, their dependency on these very same people means that their sense of being stuck is compounded. Resistance to change and consequently to the therapeutic process is considerable.

In the sessions they are reluctant to register what is being said to them and often protest that we have misunderstood. Their projected aggression leads them to experience the external world as persecutory. Likewise their potency is projected into the others around them who are now enviously attacked for their achievements. Alongside this they project into the therapist that part of themselves which they see as helpless, inadequate and unable to think. Thus, the therapist can find herself unable to make sense of their material, and consequently may feel unable to offer anything that might be useful to the patient.

I have suggested that this process can be seen frequently in patients who are married women whose husbands become the recipients of their projections. I have posited that this defence mechanism is pronounced when used in response to early environmental failure and that this is then re-enacted within the consulting room in the early stages. The therapist will need to understand and work with this means of communication before being able to make any transference interpretations which have resonance for her patient.

CHAPTER EIGHT

Psychosomatic incidents in psychotherapy

Peter Shoenberg

"It has been noted that illnesses occur more frequently at
any point of life change, even some ostensibly pleasant
or apparently trivial."

George Engel, 1975

Introduction

A man who had recently developed tinnitus, (ringing in the ears)
dreamt that he was sitting in a large arena. He was watching a
small drummer running up and down the aisles between the
rows of seats banging a drum. In the dream he tried to stop the
drummer making this noise and was reassured to find that the
man had no dangerous weapons on him.

Any physical symptom, such as this patient's tinnitus, will
arouse anxiety and a need to understand what is going on
in the body and the significance of the symptom. When
patients complain of physical symptoms during psychotherapy, a
psychotherapist may feel like a doctor without hands, for he cannot

examine his patients and establish a diagnosis as the doctor can. He is bound to experience anxiety as well as concern for his patient, (Shoenberg, 1986).

The physical symptoms of a psychosomatic illness will demand a special attention from him. In psychosomatic illness an emotional disturbance in the patient has significantly contributed to the causation of a disturbance of physical functioning and/or structure. Such disturbances when they occur during a therapy represent complex diagnostic problems and will require careful medical attention and investigation to establish their true nature. Psychosomatic disturbances of function are called somatisations. These include the effects of depression and anxiety on the body, as well as more discrete disorders such as irritable bowel syndrome, chronic fatigue syndrome, hysterical conversion reactions, hypochondriasis, neuromuscular tension states, some migrainous headaches and a variety of minor skin complaints. Psychosomatic disturbances of structure include some cases of peptic ulceration, (especially duodenal ulceration), chronic ulcerative colitis, bronchial asthma, eczema and essential hypertension. This group of conditions carries significant morbidity and some may have life threatening complications (e.g. cerebrovascular accidents in essential hypertension).

Deciding whether a physical condition is psychosomatic is difficult for the psychotherapist, even when medical help is invoked and a psychological cause has been established. That a symptom is psychosomatic means that it represents a powerful communication to the therapist of unexpressed feelings, that have either been suppressed, or denied and/or repressed, or else never expressed, as a result of early childhood disturbances in the mother/baby relationship. Some psychosomatic symptoms may be the direct expression of anxiety or depression on the body. With others, more complex mental and psychophysiological mechanisms are involved. It is still possible to make specific interpretations of certain somatisations, as for example with hysterical conversion reactions, which may choose a site of the body that has symbolic significance. With others the meaning of the symptom may be more obscure and *harder to interpret*. A therapist's desire to find a symbolic meaning in all psychosomatic symptoms may limit the scope for true understanding of what is actually happening and risk alienating the patient. With these symptoms, while it may be clear that certain psychological events have been triggers, the underlying cause may be a mixture of an *incapacity to find words for important feelings,* expressed as *gross disturbances in their psychophysiology.* These disturbances have interacted with a *physical vulnerability* resulting in physical symptoms. In many psychosomatic conditions, the precipitant of the disturbances has been the threat of a loss, or an actual or symbolic loss of a crucial relationship that has not been fully dealt with psychologically.

Both lay and medical psychotherapists should have a good general practitioner working with them. They should encourage their patients whenever they are physically ill to make full use of their doctor. Constraints of confidentiality make some psychotherapists wary of communicating with the general practitioner, except in situations of crisis, (e.g. when a patient is suicidal or might require admission to a psychiatric hospital). However, good communication between the therapist and the general practitioner makes handling of physical illness, especially a psychosomatic one occurring in therapy, easier and safer. Certainly establishing a diagnosis and cause of a physical illness can never be achieved without this additional medical help, even when the therapist is medically qualified.

Such alliances between therapist and doctor may lead to splitting in the transference.

A patient who had mild ulcerative colitis and was also taking an anxiolytic drug, propranolol, had been in therapy for some weeks. She now felt less anxious. We decided that she might usefully stop taking her medication. I wrote to her general practitioner to inform him. The following week my patient told me that her GP had actually advised her to put up the dose of the propranolol. She then asked me what she should do. I commented that perhaps she might be playing off the GP against me and suggested that she make her own decision. She decided to stop taking the propranolol (Shoenberg, 1991).

With some psychosomatic patients there may be what Winnicott described as "a scatter of the therapeutic agents", (Winnicott, 1964, p. 104).

A hypochondriacal patient, who came for help following the deaths in succession of her mother and a close brother, presented with numerous complaints for which no major physical cause could ever be found. At one point in her psychotherapy she had two GPs, a breast specialist, a gynaecologist, a gastro-enterologist, an exercise therapist, a homeopath, an osteopath and a dietician. She told me that she was terrified that she might become too dependent on me in her analysis.

Such a scatter of agents in the care of a patient may represent the fear of becoming dependent on any one single person. Winnicott also pointed out that it may be important to tolerate this diversity of therapists taking care of these patients who have multiple parts of their body that seem to be asking for help through their symptoms.

Patients in psychotherapy may be on medications (e.g. anxiolytics and antidepressants) which can have significant side effects: for example drugs like Valium (diazepam) used for anxiety may make a patient depressed; Prozac (fluoxetine), used for depression, may cause anxiety, headache and nausea. It is always helpful for the psychotherapist to be familiar with the pharmacological effects of these drugs, as well as knowing about their side effects and it is also useful to possess a good up-to-date pharmacopoeia.* Likewise, it is very important to have a clear picture of each physical condition that is under investigation and so it is also useful to refer to up-to-date medical texts that will give a simple account and aid a better understanding of a given medical condition (e.g. "Oxford Handbook of Clinical Medicine", 4th edition, 1998; or "Harrison's Principles of Internal Medicine", 15th edition, 2001).

There are advantages and disadvantages in a therapist being medically qualified. Clearly the therapist who is medical is in a stronger position to know about the implications of a given diagnosis and treatment. However, the medical therapist may also be tempted to get drawn by his patient into giving his own medical opinions which may be inappropriate technically and sometimes inaccurate.

---

*Monthly Index of Medical Specialities, published by MIMS Subscriptions, P.O. Box 43, Ruislip, Middlesex, HA4 0YT. Contains up-to-date information about drugs and their actions and side-effects.

This chapter is mainly about helping patients who present with psychosomatic symptoms during the course of their therapy. Some patients may seek psychotherapy primarily because of longstanding psychosomatic illness, such as chronic ulcerative colitis or bronchial asthma or chronic irritable bowel, but it is more common for psychotherapists to encounter acute physical symptoms which may be short-lived and may have a psychosomatic significance, so arousing concern during the course of psychotherapy: these are psychosomatic "incidents". In this chapter I would like to consider the effects of anxiety and depression on the body, then to focus on *some* of the somatising disorders that can occur in psychotherapy and finally to consider some ways in which patients react to major physical illness as part of the spectrum of disturbances involving interactions between psyche and soma in therapy.

Anxiety

In anxiety the patient may not necessarily be directly aware of his feelings. His somatic symptoms are caused by over-activity of the sympathetic nervous system. Wolff lists the somatic symptoms as follows: cardiovascular symptoms may include palpitations and chest pain. Respiratory symptoms may include breathlessness, over-breathing with air hunger. Over-breathing may result in dizziness and tingling sensations caused by changes in the blood gases resulting in alkalosis. In the gastro-intestinal system a patient may complain of a dry mouth, butterflies in the stomach, or diarrhoea. In the genito-urinary system a patient may complain of increased frequency of micturition, urgency of micturition and there may be impotence and loss of libido. Sweating commonly occurs in the palms of the hands or in the armpits. In addition, the inability to relax leading to muscle tension, may result in a tension headache or tension in the neck and shoulder. Sleep may be disturbed with initial insomnia and interrupted sleep (Wolff, 1990, p. 159). These symptoms may occur singly or in combination with each other.

An example of palpitations in psychotherapy

A young man developed palpitations after his mother's death

from a heart attack. These palpitations represented his identification with his mother's own heart condition and his way of expressing anxiety over his unresolved grief. Although we discussed the meaning of these palpitations in the session, they resolved after his own GP gave him a good physical check-up and reassured him that there was nothing physically wrong with his heart.

Depression

Many patients complain of physical symptoms during a depression and they may even consider that these have caused their depression or may not be aware they are depressed. A patient may neglect to take care of himself and will appear tired, with a poor quality of sleep which has been interrupted throughout the night (he may find he is waking early in the morning in a more severe depression). In very severe depression the patient may also be slowed down. In the gastro-intestinal system there may be constipation. Headaches and ringing in the ears (tinnitus) may occur. Back pain, weakness and fatigue may be part of the picture. Sometimes facial pain may occur linked to recent dental treatment (all described in Wolff, 1990, p. 201).

A depression may also exacerbate the suffering caused by pre-existing somatic symptoms and be a cause of excessive anxiety about them (see section on hypochondriasis). Recurrent infections occurring during psychotherapy may also represent some important communication from a patient to the therapist about his emotional vulnerability and his immune system, linked to underlying unresolved depressive conflicts. These conflicts can produce a poorer immune response, particularly at times of major loss and grief. A severe depression will probably require additional psychiatric help.

Hysterical conversion symptoms

Although hysterical conversion symptoms are nowadays rare as a direct cause for a patient seeking psychotherapy, occasionally patients during psychotherapy can develop transient conversion symptoms. These may include difficulty in swallowing or problems with phonation and occasionally other neurological symptoms such as transient alterations in sensation, for example, the development of pins and needles on one side of the body or psychogenic pains. The hallmark of all these symptoms is that they have no underlying neurological basis.

An example of hysterical difficulty in swallowing occurring during a break in therapy

One patient whom I was seeing for once weekly psychotherapy who had presented with a prolonged grief reaction following the death of her father, was a nurse in her early twenties who had had a close but ambivalent relationship to the father. After his death, she could not deal with this loss. She knew there had been difficulties in the relationship which stemmed from childhood experiences to do with the earlier, more significant loss of her mother when she was five. After this bereavement she had formed an over-intense attachment to her father. This had been spoilt by his second marriage to a woman with whom she was to have a poor relationship. Later, when she fell in love and married her husband, who was training to be a surgeon, her father was not able to accept him. The young couple had a small child, aged one. Therapy with her initially proceeded well during which time she told me much about her past. She told me about her difficulties in her relationship with her husband, of whom she was easily jealous.

At this point in the therapy I took a holiday of 2 weeks. When I returned I was worried to hear from her husband that she wanted to see me urgently because she felt she needed to be admitted to hospital. When I saw her, she told me that she had been frightened of harming her baby while I was away. She was sure that she and her baby should be protected from this happening by her being hospitalised. However, during the session she calmed down. She told me how on the day and the time when we would have met in the first week when I had been away, she had suddenly found herself unable to swallow. This difficulty in swallowing had gone on for a number of minutes before she had driven over to the Casualty Department at the hospital where her husband was working. He was called to see her and he reassured her and the episode of choking disappeared. We were both struck by the fact that it had happened precisely at the moment when the session would have occurred, and it had not recurred after that time. It was clear to me that her hope in the attack was for some sort of an understanding. In staking her claim for understanding from her husband, there was self-punishment built into her symptom formation so that, with him, her despair was translated into the exaggerated act of choking. Whereas with myself this despair was communicated as her depression.

So I was able to see how there had been an hysterical element in her behaviour which had escaped me until now, and which gave the account of her baby an exaggerated quality. This had more to do with her demand for my attention in the transference as her missing parent, either father or mother. I never admitted her to hospital.

Many months later she told me that she had, indeed, exaggerated her feelings about hurting the baby and, in fact, had only slapped her baby very lightly on the occasion when I was away. The transformation of her symptomatology from depression transferentially manifested towards myself, as her therapist, to the conversion symptom that she showed her husband as a doctor, emphasises how a somatisation can catch a therapist unawares as an enactment of transference issues during a separation (Shoenberg, 1975).

Hypochondriasis

Major hypochondriasis is a rare initial presentation in patients seeking psychotherapy, but can occur in a minor way during the course of treatment. Wolff describes the features of hypochondriasis as follows: the patient presents with all the features of extreme worrying. He is troubled by unpleasant thoughts, about the possibility of disease or malfunctions of parts of the body, and sometimes this is in association with an actual physical illness; his worry is quite out of proportion to the severity of the underlying condition, and it does not respond to reassurance. The common symptoms that cause worry are pain, and preoccupations with the heart, and with the respiratory system, and gastro-intestinal disturbances (Wolff, 1990, pp. 184–186).

A psychotherapist dealing with hypochondriacal preoccupations is bound to be worried about what really is the matter. It is always important that a patient first seeks a medical opinion. When it is clear that the source of the symptom is not based in a severe physical pathology, but represents an exaggerated concern about a relatively minor physical problem, or even an absent physical problem, it is worth considering the underlying anxiety and depression in the patient. Commonly a hypochondriacal fear is linked to anxieties about death or dying from terminal or incurable illnesses, such as cancer and these phantasies are linked to fears of being abandoned and of dying alone. Ideally, such symptoms should be medically investigated conservatively, that is, not beyond a certain point. A lay psychotherapist will be vulnerable in this area of his work, and it is always helpful to discuss such cases with medically qualified colleagues, as well as arranging for their assessment by the GP and/or relevant medical specialist.

An example of hypochondriacal reaction to a forthcoming break in therapy

A 50-year old, married, office worker had been seeing me for some years because of chronic irritable bowel syndrome, exacerbated after the death of a close, older, male friend. She had a background of a difficult relationship with her mother, who had died some while before she had come to see me, and an ambivalent relationship with her father. Her childhood had been troubled by many separations between the ages of 8 and 11, during the Second World War, when she was frequently evacuated to stay with various foster parents. These separations were frightening for her and compounded the earlier cumulative trauma of her relationship with the mother. She now had a poor relationship with her husband, who was an unsuccessful businessman.

In the therapy she seemed to form an angry but suspicious

dependence on me, mirroring both the difficult relationship with her father and perhaps a more empty relationship with her mother. After some years of work together she recovered completely from her irritable bowel. I had to take a long period of leave and shortly after telling her about this, she developed a feeling of tension in her chest with pain radiating down her arm. She had gone to her GP who had not been able to find anything wrong with her; however she remained afraid that there might be something more sinister wrong with her such as a tumour. She felt her pain had been made worse by my telling her about my going away, and linked it to her sense that, apart from her husband and myself, there was no-one in her life left to help her. I was also worried that there might be a medical as well as a psychological reason for the pain, and encouraged her to get further investigations. She went to a local medical specialist who arranged an x-ray. This was normal. However, she was still frightened about her symptoms. She told me a dream of being on holiday in France. She also reported quarrelling with her husband because he had failed to engage with the therapist that she had so much wanted him to see. I interpreted her wish to try to resolve all her difficulties in her relationship with him before my going away.

She now went to see an osteopath for treatment of her pain. She cancelled the session with me. When she came for the next session, she told me it had been *my* fault that she had got the pain, because *I* had caused her so much distress by going away. She now cancelled another session, but by the time we reached our last session before my going away, her chest and arm pains had completely resolved.

The pains indeed were a somatic representation of her anger and distress about this forthcoming long separation in the analysis, but it was she who came to this conclusion, before I could, because of the need for a careful medical assessment of this problem.

Neuromuscular tension states

These include a wide variety of syndromes produced by the effect of tension on the body. They may be linked to muscular tension arising from pain in physically vulnerable areas of the body, such as those caused by degenerative diseases of the spine. Sometimes there is no underlying physical lesion, as is the case with tension headaches: here the muscles at the front and back of the skull can go into spasm and produce a continuous dull pain directly related to the stressful situation. Such pains should be carefully physically investigated to exclude headaches produced by damage to the underlying structures. In a tension headache there is a persistent contraction of muscles of the head and neck. It is almost always directly linked to emotional tension, anxiety and depression leading to the painful muscular contraction and it often occurs on both sides of the head. It can start in the neck, the back or the front of the head. It may start as a dull ache, but can become more severe and even throbbing. Often attacks last all day, and rarely they occur daily for days or weeks, which arouses further anxiety and tension. Unlike the headaches of migraine, there is no warning aura or other neurological disturbance and nausea and vomiting are rare (all discussed in Wolff and Shoenberg, 1990).

An example of a tension headache linked to the stress of overwork

A patient in the third year of his analysis developed strange persistent pains in the head, which were described as tense feelings at the front on both sides, not associated with nausea. The headache had occurred at a stressful time in his career when he was changing from his field of childcare, which was very demanding and doing an additional training in social work. He was worried that the headaches might have a more ominous significance. However, it was clear that the amount of work he was doing was producing resentment, distress and anxiety, linked to memories of being exploited by his mother in childhood, as well as an identification with mother's own migrainous headaches. I advised him to go to his GP for an assessment. He never did, but the headache went away and proved to be of no major physical significance. These daily headaches represented a warning to him about the amount of pressure he had placed himself under.

Migrainous headaches

Such a warning to the patient produced by the physical symptom can give him a helpful indication that something should be done about the situation which he is in. George Groddeck, the psychotherapist and physician, was one of the first psychotherapists to point out that a physical illness could have psychological meaning (Groddeck, 1977). However clearly one may appreciate the psychological factors in any somatisation, it may be unwise to make interpretations prematurely about its significance.

An example of migrainous headaches as an expression of unverbalised anger

A patient developed nocturnal headaches during the course of a very unhappy marriage to an unfaithful husband, when he forced her to give up her career to look after his mother. She decided as a result of these headaches that she could no longer put up with the poor relationship that she was in, which was now making her feel physically ill: she ended her marriage.

Originally she had been unable to leave him until the development of severe frightening shock-like headaches which woke her in the night. The headaches had often been preceded by nightmares. Sleep studies performed by a medical specialist suggested that she was developing a form of breathing difficulty in the night, causing changes in her blood gases, which resulted in migrainous headaches. She told me at this point in the therapy that she had, as a small child, suffered with frightening nightmares from which she woke screaming, after a much loved nanny had been forced to leave the house by her mother, who had been jealous. Her mother herself had also suffered with bad headaches. She had had a poor relationship with both parents but especially with the mother, who had very much neglected her as a small child. In early childhood she had been sent away to boarding school. She then had developed bad migrainous headaches herself.

She had difficulty in expressing her anger in general and in particular towards her husband. It was only after the development of the headaches that she began to get directly angry with him and then decided to leave him. This led to a complete remission from the headaches and a far greater sense of independence in her and a greater capacity to express her emotions more directly.

This case history taught me how very often the significance of a given somatisation as a representation of past conflicts and identifications with physical illness experienced in childhood, may only emerge at a late stage. With this patient we did not arrive at such a meaningful reconstruction of this physical disturbance until this somatisation was on its way out. Also, this case illustrates how a somatisation often represents emotions which the patient has great difficulty in expressing. In some psychosomatic patients there may be a generalised difficulty in finding words for their feelings which has been called "alexithymia", resulting from early difficulties in learning to process and regulate affects, stemming from very early failures in the mother/infant relationship (Taylor et al., 1997)

Some minor skin conditions
presenting in psychotherapy

Mood changes may influence the function of the skin. Shame and embarrassment can cause dilatation of the blood vessels, making people blush. Anxiety and fear may lead to constriction of blood vessels, which can cause pallor and increased sweating. Excessive sweating may occur and also be a source of embarrassment and anxiety.

Itching, which is also called pruritus, is often due to a physical cause such as eczema, which is itself a structural psychosomatic disorder, but psychological factors can also be directly causative. Psychogenic itching may be generalised or localised to one region of the body such as the neck, genital region or anus. Sometimes it may have to do with difficulty in expressing anger and frustration and a patient may develop itching and scratch himself instead. Severe and repeated scratching, in turn, not only causes itching, but skin blemishes, leading sometimes to hardening of the skin and a localised dermatitis (neurodermatitis) (all discussed in Wolff and Shoenberg, 1990).

A case of neurodermatitis

A patient who had lost her mother in her late adolescence because the mother committed suicide and subsequently lost a younger brother who committed suicide on the anniversary of the mother's death, developed a red rash with blisters around her mouth produced by scratching. She said herself that when she got this rash it felt as if all the pain and hurt from her childhood and adolescence was expressing itself in this angry skin eruption.

Psychosomatic incidents as regressive phenomena

In 1923 George Groddeck wrote in his classic paper "The Meaning of Illness" about the unconscious forces at work that might make someone fall, leading to a fracture of their femur. He wrote of the person's intent,

> I am helpless, help me, you who are grown up. Have sympathy, help me, ease my pain. I am suffering innocently. You are obliged to do it. Look here, I am lying, I am a child; you are standing, you are walking, you are obliged to help the child. [Groddeck, 1923, 1925]

This description is about the secondary gain involved in this accident and its consequences and it highlights the relevance of the role of regression. Very often in psychosomatic incidents and conditions we can see that there is evidence of the use of the physical symptom to allow the person to have some sort of regression. Most of us have probably experienced this on some occasions when we go off sick from work and feel a degree of relief and a sense of comfort from knowing that we have earned the right to be looked after. A schizoid patient who develops a mild infection, such as influenza, may experience this in an even more positive way as some sort of reunifying of his mind and body, when normally he experiences himself as living very much in a mental world, split off from his bodily experiences. Winnicott emphasises this in his paper on psychosomatic illness (Winnicott, 1964). In the hypochondriacal patient the experience of illness may have particular significance in terms of regression to a time when he experienced more care and physical contact from his mother as a result of being ill, and this may play a very significant role in his transference to the therapist.

Note on physical illnesses acquiring secondary psychological meaning

It is not uncommon for patients in psychotherapy, when they develop a major physical illness, to attribute psychological causes and meanings to their illness. They may feel guilt and self-reproach for having developed the illness. They may interpret their illness as a form of punishment or failure on their part. The patient may see his physical illness as a token of an underlying psychological weakness. As we learn more about illness in general and more about lifestyle habits that can lead to dangerous physical conditions such as coronary artery disease, bowel cancer and so on, patients may feel more responsible for factors which have caused the development of their condition, even if in reality they are actually quite out of their control.

When patients develop potentially lethal conditions such as cancer, it is important to try to work with their fears and appreciate the significance of these, especially when they have a depressive tinge. Physical illness itself may produce psychological symptoms for organic reasons, such as chronic fatigue and depression. Even minor illnesses such as a prolonged viral infection can also produce depression and fatigue in the recovery period.

Example of a depressive evaluation of a physical illness

A woman whose marriage broke up in her mid fifties developed bleeding from the rectum caused by ulcerative colitis. Associated with the bleeding at the onset of her colitis she developed severe constipation as well. She reported a dream to her therapist after receiving the diagnosis of colitis, in which she was presenting her mother with the contents of a purse given to her by her ex-husband. The contents consisted of hard faecal pellets from her constipated colon. She thought as she gave the contents to her mother, "Now this is all I am worth". The dream expressed the patient's guilt and anxiety about her recent loss of her partner, but also represented an unfavourable commentary on this new physical condition.

Conclusion

This short account of psychosomatic incidents and psychological reactions to physical illness in psychoanalytic psychotherapy is by no means comprehensive. It is clearly important that each therapist pays great attention to the body with its potential physical problems and their links to the mind and emotions.

Psychosomatic incidents do not necessarily only have to refer to the physical symptoms that a patient has, but also to the movements, gestures and postures that may be taken up by his body, including facial and other physical expressions of emotion. Some patients with despair may be particularly prone to damage themselves through accidents. Other patients may make quieter communications by the way in which they choose to lie on the couch, the way in which they hold their head or the way in which they look at the therapist. All these communications are as relevant as the speech content of the session, but commenting on them may be problematic as Winnicott found:

> With a silent patient, a man of 25 years, I once interpreted the movement of his fingers as his hand lay closed across his chest. He said to me: "If you start interpreting that sort of thing, then I shall have to transfer that sort of activity to something else which does not show". In other words, he was pointing out to me that unless he had verbalised his communication, it was not for me to make comment. [Winnicott, 1968, p. 207]

The psychotherapist, although he is always preoccupied with the psychological aspects of his patient, should always be concerned with his patient's physical wellbeing and the relevance of this to his psychosomatic health, as much as his colleague in general practice is concerned to understand the psychological issues affecting the physical illnesses he has to deal with. Psychosomatic incidents may or may not "join in the conversation" (Breuer and Freud, 1893–1895) with the psychotherapist, but they are always worth exploring in psychotherapy, even when simple interpretations of their meaning are not possible.

CHAPTER NINE

Psychosis as jack in the box

Dianne Campbell Lefevre

"I am, they say, a darkling pool
Where huge and cunning lurks a fool
Childish and monstrous, untaught of time,
Still wallowing in primeval slime.
All powerful he with fang and claw
To fill his red capacious maw,
And not a thousand thousand years
Have eased his belly, stilled his fears.
But ever with dim consuming fire
Swirl the slow eddies of desire
About his sprawling limbs, and lull
The torments of his brutish skull.
He is most merciless, lone and proud
There in the scaly darkness bowed,
And sleeps, and eats, and lusts, and cries,
And never lives and never dies.
Nay, but above this stagnant night
The lovely highways of the light
Sweep on with winds and dawning flowers
And stoop to touch its midnight hours.
If I am he, I'm also one

With all that's brave beneath the sun,
With lovers' singing, and great tall trees,
And the white glory of the seas.
What of this silence, so there stay
Child's laughter to the end of day?
And what of dark, if on the hill
Eve is a burning opal still?"

Barrington Gates.
"Abnormal Psychology" In Behold the Dreamer. (1984)

The effects of the psychoses on the lives of many sufferers are devastating. The results of treatments of the psychoses in sophisticated centres around the world are disappointing. The most hopeful treatment area seems to be the possibility of arresting or reversing the progress of the illness at an early stage, thus preventing chronicity. Clinicians need to devote time to think together about these illnesses. Theorising without clinical experience is often misleading. I believe Bion said concept without intuition is empty and intuition without concept is blind. Intuition is developed and refined by the hard work involved in clinical experience and, in particular, in the understanding of the countertransference.

A little thought about the nature of psychosis brings all sorts of questions to mind. Why is the psychotic process so tyrannical, vicious and threatening? Why does it succeed in holding the patient in its thrall? Why can one not simply explain why a delusion (e.g. "I am Crassus who hanged Spartacus upside down") is out of touch with reality, since the individual, while remaining convinced of the delusion, nevertheless understands perfectly well that he has to see the psychiatrist, collect his tablets, buy food from the shops and so on. This otherwise sensible individual may not object to having two people claiming to be Jesus on the ward or have any quarrel with being Hitler and Jesus—"It is strange that I am a Jew and Hitler" said one patient. Why the disregard for time? For example—I have quoted this elsewhere—"I was Alexander the Great and now I can't get Dot to make the tea!" (LeFevre & Morrison, 1997) The same patient was anxiously pacing up and down worrying that his therapist might have booked another appointment in his session time.

Although the consulting room would rarely see the patient with a severe or a recurring schizophrenic illness, subtle shades of psychosis are frequently present. I suspect that an active, ongoing psychotic process is often missed, not least because the sufferer feels tyrannised by the psychotic process and cannot reveal it. In any event, some understanding of the more florid illness can be helpful in understanding all patients—and ourselves (Richards, 1993; Sinason, 1993).

An unfortunate consequence of missing the presence of a psychotic process may be a patient who disappears from therapy, terrified by the nameless dread which is impregnated with futility, hopelessness and despair. This dread (often mistakenly viewed as anxiety) may precede suicide and/or the delusional mood. In line with the title of this chapter, this might be followed by a most undesirable Jack popping out of the box in the form of death (that is dreaded) (Winnicott, 1974) by suicide, or assault/murder as an aspect of the Death Constellation (Hyatt-Williams, 1998) or frank psychosis and admission to hospital.

I have found that the models of psychosis which ring true and are of most help in treating severely ill patients in all the above modalities, are those that assume a distinction between psychotic and nonpsychotic personalities—hence the rather gaudy image of the Jack in the box. However Jack does not always leap out and punch one on the nose with a suicide, homicide or dramatic need for admission to hospital. He may lurk inside the box for variable periods of time, blend in with the wallpaper or confuse the observer with a figure/ ground appearance which makes one ask who is it who is mad?!

Whatever the situation Jack, and the box, and the environment of the box need to be examined. The DSM-IV (2000) and the ICD-10 (1992) allow for this in offering several diagnostic categories—in effect inviting a diagnosis of the psychotic and nonpsychotic aspects of the patient. In fact the British Diagnostic Manual, the ICD10, recommends that "clinicians should follow the general rule of recording as many diagnoses as are necessary."

Assessment

Hence, a full psychiatric assessment (including a detailed history and account of phenomenology past and present) is helpful, if not essential, but is not adequate to establish the structural diagnosis necessary to clarify the predominant personality organisation (Kernberg, 1999). For this, one needs a full psychodynamic assessment done by a psychotherapist experienced in working with psychosis. Coltart (1987) makes the point that it is useful to know as much about the patient as possible.

In the case of the psychiatric assessment the predisposing–precipitating–perpetuating factors, all with reference to the biological–psychological–social status need to be fully explored. This approach integrates pharmacological, psychological and social therapies; the reasons for it have been summarised by Alanen (1997) in his account of the Finnish experience of treatment of schizophrenia and related disorders.

Specially careful assessment of suspicious symptoms occurring in teenagers can prove invaluable. There is evidence that adding psychological treatment to the usual drug and milieu treatments at the first signs of schizophrenia in adolescents and in adults may prevent ongoing florid illness (McGorry, 2000; Falloon et al., 1996). When one considers the damage and suffering caused by chronic psychosis it seems impossible to exaggerate the importance of being aware of the need for early detection and treatment.

A difficulty is that in young patients the prodromal symptoms of schizophrenia, such as reduced concentration, anxiety and sleep disturbance can frequently occur in ordinarily stressful situations. Early symptoms of psychosis may be rather mild and nonspecific, such as peculiar behaviour, loss of expression of feelings, speech that is difficult to follow and so on (Yung & McGorry, 1996).

Psychotherapy for psychosis?

I go along with the view that psychotherapeutic treatment of patients who are too severely disturbed to participate in a standard psychoanalysis can be very useful (Alanen, 1997; Cullberg et al., 2000). Cullberg's pilot study offering "need adapted treatment" to first illness schizophrenics has shown positive results in that it is suggested that early integrative treatment (pharmacological, family therapy and psychotherapy when indicated and possible) may prevent chronicity. He also points out that this would make financial sense. Some practitioners might correctly regard themselves as having insufficient experience of severe mental illness, or insufficient training in psychoanalytical psychotherapy to take on a patient with an entrenched psychotic illness. Kernberg (1999) has suggested additional training for psychoanalysts in order to develop the wider flexibility of technique necessary in severe mental illness.

In addition to a requirement that the therapist has special training and experience, in the interest of safety, patients with a severe psychotic illness should be seen with the backing and cooperation of a hospital with in-patient facilities and an emergency response team, an agreement which is not always easy to arrange in today's NHS. Thus, in the case of the expected serious regression, negative therapeutic reactions or increased activity of the psychotic process where damaging acting out, such as suicide or homicide might take place, admission can be arranged by the psychiatric team without too much disruption of the transference relationship between patient and therapist.

It is not always the case that severe mental illness is detected or is predictable at a full psychiatric or psychodynamic assessment.

A patient Les attended a hospital out-patient clinic for over a year and was seen by more than one Consultant Psychiatrist and several junior doctors who treated an apparent mood distur- bance with antidepressants. An art therapist became aware that Les had olfactory and visual hallucinations and felt controlled by a tyrannical force, named by the patient, Dob, about which Les was terrified to speak. Alerting the psychiatric team was of no avail as the right questions, at the right time were never asked, and Les was apparently able to function at home. So it was assumed that all was well. A full psychodynamic assessment revealed a very long standing, psychotic process Dob, which took the form of a sadistic inner figure, which terrorised the patient by giving frightening content to visual and auditory hallucinations and by convincing Les of life threatening delusional beliefs. The psychotic process, Dob, functioned alongside a traumatised but relatively robust nonpsychotic personality with borderline features. This patient is making good progress in weekly psychoanalytical psychotherapy and is now on minimal medication.

Because of its close relationship with psychosis, it is important to be on the look out for Obsessive Compulsive Disorder (OCD), which is easily missed and often only detectable in the early stages by direct questioning about the relevant symptoms. It is a difficult condition to treat with biological treatment and/or in psycho-analytical psychotherapy. OCD is relatively frequent in patients with first episode schizophrenia and may have some protective effect on some schizophrenic symptoms (Poyurovsky et al., 1999) There have been a number of recent reports on OCD occurring prior to or with schizophrenic illnesses, suggesting for example, that there may be a distinct subtype of schizophrenia wherein patients show poor cognitive functioning (Berman et al., 1998) and that persistent OCD symptoms within a schizophrenic illness are a powerful predictor of poor prognosis (Fenton et al., 1986). Clearly these factors would influence the type of treatment one might suggest or offer.

Although the differences between obsessive ruminations and delusion are sometimes clinically obvious, that is not always the case.

A man's obsessional rumination that he had cancer of the breast very gradually shaded into a delusion that he did indeed have cancer and that this had been visited upon him by an outside force over which he had no control (passivity). This further developed into a florid schizophrenic illness.

The usefulness of a model of psychosis

The models of psychosis developed by Bion, Grotstein, (who extrapolates on Fairbairn's theories of Object Relations and Winnicott's work), M. Robbins and others, assume the existence of a psychotic and a nonpsychotic personality. To know, very broadly, what to expect if therapy is offered, it is helpful to know something of the nature of the nonpsychotic personality. This aspect of the individual at least in part is wanting to engage in a process called therapy, which in theory should be a helpful, healing process. A relatively strong nonpsychotic personality is better able to resist being overwhelmed by the psychotic process whose hatred of reality (which includes the need for and connection with the therapist) will inevitably lead to a stormy course.

It is interesting that some people with florid and multiple symptoms of psychosis are nevertheless able to manage their lives outside hospital, sometimes even coping with some kind of a job. Other people who show very little evidence of psychotic symptomatology, may be unable to care for themselves and may not be able to perform any formal work.

This must have something to do with the nature and the relative strengths of the psychotic and nonpsychotic personalities.

A patient with catatonic schizophrenia, a condition now rarely seen, was electively mute and would stand in one position with his head bowed most of the time. Where there could have been a verbalisation of anger, he defecated where he stood. Very little communication was possible.

It appears that in such patients there is very little accessible nonpsychotic personality. The depleted nonpsychotic aspects of the patient are overwhelmed by the active psychotic process. Occasionally, individuals with severe psychotic illness are discovered unwashed, in a state of malnutrition and dehydration and living in unhealthy circumstances, unable to take care of themselves because they are so out of touch with reality.

At the other end of the scale there are people who have active psychotic symptoms who are able to lead fairly ordinary lives and who do not appear to be particularly unusual.

Interaction between ontogenetic and phylogenetic factors

Unfortunately there is not the space in this chapter to do justice to this important subject. Understanding the subtle interaction between ontogeny and phylogeny can help to understand the usefulness and limitations of the psychotherapeutic aspect of treatment of severe mental illness.

Examination of the families and the lives of individuals with severe mental illness suggests that the development of such mental illness requires a convergence of multiple factors, organic (including genetic) and environmental.

Organic brain damage, (genetic, biochemical, structural, traumatic or toxic) gives rise to the potential for perceptual abnormalities (visual, olfactory, auditory or tactile) which appear under certain circumstances, much in the same way as the brain damage in epilepsy results in fits occurring when certain conditions prevail. The raw hallucinatory experiences described by Lishman (1980) are given meaning by the patient's life experience (Hamilton, 1976).

In psychosis, circumstances which seem to trigger or to worsen the perceptual experiences appear to take the form of unpalatable reality, frequently the reality of needing others. The complex nature of the delusional system is more easily seen as derived from the patient's life experience.

A patient who had a schizophrenic illness with elaborate symptoms including clear hallucinations showed improvement and increasing strength of the nonpsychotic personality over several years of psychoanalytical psychotherapy. After about 4 months when she had been taken off all medication the patient suffered a devastating life event which precipitated a sense of loss and grieving. The hallucinatory experiences returned for a while, initially as quiet voices, later clear hallucinatory voices and later still there was an intermittent, infrequent return of the malevolent, tyrannical (delusional) force which instructed the patient to pay attention to the voices and not to the therapist.

The phylogenetic factors involved in the development of schizophrenia spectrum disorders have been put forward by Crow (1991, 1997) and Horrobin (1999) amongst others. Crow relates the origins to the speciation event, the origins of language and cerebral asymmetries, Horrobin to brain fatty acid abnormalities (Peet et al., 1999; Puri et al., 2000; Mellor et al., 1996).

Alongside this and of great importance is evidence that experience (including psychotherapy) can change both developing and mature brains (Greenough, 1987). The Hawthorn Project (LeFevre & Morrison, 1997; Lefevre, 1999) demonstrated that even "long-stay" in-patients with chronic psychoses demonstrably benefited from weekly, analytically informed group psychotherapy.

Gabbard's (1997) review paper, with useful references, states in the conclusion that "dynamic therapy ... appears to work by influencing the functioning of the brain and is therefore as much of a "medical" treatment as pharmacotherapy. It also adds a critical dimension of meaning to psychiatric treatment, a dimension of "mind" that the "brain" cannot do without...". Kandel (1999) argues that developing a closer relationship with biology in general and cognitive neuroscience in particular is central to the development of psychoanalysis.

Phylogeny may account for the fact of severe mental illness, if and when it is established, but not the detail of it. The interplay between ontogenetic and phylogenetic factors forms part of the more recent psychoanalytical models. The relative importance of ontogeny is in the ascendancy following the results of the human genome project.

Psychoanalytical models

There would not be space in this chapter to write an overview of psychoanalytic models of psychosis. Robbins (1993) and Alanen (1999) have both given succinct summaries of biological and psychological contributions to severe mental illness.

Devising a model is an epistemological exercise. Its purpose is to find words that give meaning and coherence to behaviours, thought processes and affective experiences which arise in order to deal with or to express the results of biological and psychological assaults or stresses on the organism. It usually assumes a mind brain interaction. It may be a guide to the most helpful treatment designed to secure the best possible outcome in terms of function and of subjective comfort. It may help to set this series of behaviours, arising from psychological and biological damage or deviation into the context of society and culture.

The model may include the biological and psychosocial origins and evolution of mental illness, and predictor factors. Each therapist has to find his/her own language and the tradition with its models of therapy that makes most sense. I use a mixture of psychodynamic models.

The model itself is a symbolic representation, not a concrete fact.

Freud hoped that he would find neuroanatomical or neurophysio-
logical correlates to his psychological models. Interestingly, the
work of Dr Mark and Karen Solms (Kaplan-Solms & Solms, 2000) is
correlating anatomical areas with psychological function. However,
needless to say, there is no real patch over the rent in the ego (Freud,
1923b), the ego is not an anatomical structure. However, I found this
particular description enlightening as the implication of the
defensive nature of the psychotic process made sense of what I
was seeing in the hospital setting taking place in patients with acute
and chronic psychoses. A brief vignette might illustrate the arising
of the defence.

> A patient on a locked ward was terrified, unable to communicate
> and was wandering around looking suspiciously at his sur-
> roundings, not unlike a captured wild animal about to explode.
> He would not relinquish a weapon he had acquired. The staff
> were afraid too—experiencing his fear and a rational fear of the
> possible consequences. A sudden delusional realisation, which
> in later weeks was elaborated into complex delusional ideation
> triggered the expected attack. After his "realisation" (primary
> delusion) was experienced, his terrible sense of dread, futility
> and hopelessness left him and he had a sense that his anger had
> a purpose, albeit in a rather dream-like state. The "scaffolding"
> of the delusional ideation which offered an explanation for his
> fear, protected him against the agony of experiencing the
> annihilation anxiety accompanying disintegration.

> The experienced staff member who had been with him wept
> later, saying that to experience countertransferentially some-
> thing of the patient's dread and terror at such close quarters was
> overwhelming. He too was relieved at the point where he had to
> act to defend himself.

This kind of primary delusion can recur and this is one of the
many reasons why seeing very ill people in private practice without
a hospital geographically close, may be unwise.

All psychoanalytical models of psychosis have derived at least in
part from Freud's theories, although he was even pessimistic about
the treatment of narcissistic disorders. A footnote in "Neurosis and

Psychosis" (Freud, 1923b) mentions his unfinished work "Splitting of the Ego in the Process of Defence". This idea of splitting of the ego was developed later by Object Relations theorists.

Gill (1967) expanded on the nature of the id and primary process which through a failure of repression determines the content and form of psychotic material. He described the characteristics as:

1. Exemption from mutual contradictions (e.g. "I am Crassus who hanged Spartacus upside down, I am a patient in a psychiatric hospital".)
2. Timelessness e.g. "I used to be Alexander the Great and now I can't get Dot to make the tea".
3. Replacement of internal by external reality—secondary process takes into consideration the external world, primary process does not. ("I (Hitler) attempted suicide (yesterday) because I knew they were going to get me for all the harm I did in the war".)
4. Those characterising primary process, i.e. condensation, displacement and the replacement of symbolic representation by symbolic equation.

Harry Stack Sullivan was an early worker in the field of psychosis and some of his ideas were taken up by Harold Searles (1987), whose important and pioneering work is enriched by an abundance of clinical experience and enlivened by an unusual, refreshing and invigorating frankness, particularly in his accounts of countertransference, the skilful use of which was crucial in his treatment of severe mental disorder.

A major step in the understanding of psychosis and severe mental disorder was taken by the British Objects Relations school. Melanie Klein dated the onset of object relating back to birth and proposed an inner world built up of introjects consisting of composites of the object, ego representative and affect. First part objects in the paranoid schizoid position and later whole objects in the depressive position could be defensively expelled into another person in an attempt to control that person/object and later reintrojected.

The emphasis placed by Klein (1975) on the use of projective identification in primitive mental states adds a great deal of understanding to phenomena encountered in severe mental disorder and is consistent with the idea of a split between psychotic and nonpsychotic personality. The importance of projective identification as a developmental process, a defence, a mode of communication, a primitive form of object relating has been particularly well described by Ogden (1979).

Fairbairn (1981), although not particularly associated with work with psychosis, has been of great importance for my developing some understanding of the way patients present themselves in different ways, including the psychotic nonpsychotic split. I shall include his contribution with that of Grotstein.

Bion (1967, Chap. 5) probably made the greatest step forward in the understanding of psychotic mechanisms. He made the simple but important statement that there is no such thing as a psychotic/ schizophrenic. There is only a person with a psychotic/schizophrenic illness. He described the hatred of reality in psychosis that leads to splitting of the ego into minute fragments which are projected into outside objects and impregnated with cruelty. They are seen as persecutors and give content to hallucinations. He emphasised the ever widening divergence between psychotic and nonpsychotic personality until there is an unbridgeable gulf between them, saying: "I do not think real progress with psychotic patients is likely to take place until due weight is given to the nature of the divergence between the psychotic and nonpsychotic personalities."

Bion dated the initial pathology leading to the development of a psychotic illness to very early in life. A good psychiatric history from the patient and the family often confirms this. Parents sometimes recall abnormalities in patients as babies and patients themselves often recall the psychotic process bothering them long before the illness was formally recognised.

Bion (1967, Chap. 4) described the preconditions for schizophrenic mechanisms to develop as a preponderance of destructive over libidinal impulses (love turns to sadism and hatred), hatred of reality internal and external (hence attacks on perception, hatred of needing the therapist or any lively contact with the therapist, such as loving, hating etc.), dread of imminent annihilation and a premature and precipitate formation of object relations (a thin, premature tenacious transference).

The intensely dependent relationship with the therapist, with affects arising, leads to multiple splits and overactive projective identification with a confusional state developing as described by Rosenfeld (1984) and in order to escape this, a fleeing from the therapeutic relationship. So contact with the therapist is followed by the risk of a take-over by the psychotic personality and a turning away from any alive contact with the therapist.

Such contact as there is taking place, is often with a very damaged nonpsychotic personality, with borderline and narcissistic features, of the type described by Kernberg (1980) in his classification of borderline conditions. Very quickly the contact, which satisfies a healthy libidinal need, has to be destroyed by the reality hating psychotic personality which is felt to lead an independent and uncontrolled existence.

This is sometimes experienced by the therapist as a switch from a two person human relationship, to a coming face-to-face with an inanimate object. This turning away from a healthy contact leads to a dilemma. Talking in therapy to anything other than the nonpsychotic personality is the equivalent of talking to a TV screen and likely to lead nowhere.

The dilemma for the patient is whether to give in to the tyrannical psychotic personality whose hatred of reality and pressing demand for secrecy and loyalty from the patient, can lead at worst to precipitate suicide or homicide. Alternatively, he must suffer being in contact with the therapist with the attendant pain of awareness of need and the inevitable disappointment—both transferential and in reality. This is not under the patient's conscious control.

At these moments, for the therapist, the countertransference must be a guiding force. The task is to accurately determine psychotic and nonpsychotic elements and feed back this information to the nonpsychotic personality when it is available. This helps to hold on to a state where thought is possible.

It is my belief that, working in alliance with the nonpsychotic personality does not mean discounting the psychic apparatus as having a potentially unitary nature. If one observes the point of anxiety, when the patient suddenly moves from a state where he is in contact with reality to one where there is a loss of contact with the therapist and with reality (i.e. the move into a psychotic state), one finds invariably that it is generated by contact with the therapist which is above an acceptable threshold of intensity. This contact reflects the reality of needing the therapist, being angry with the therapist or any sort of closeness found in an intimate relationship. All interpretations must be addressed to the nonpsychotic personality (Bion, 1992, p. 176) which has some capacity for thinking and which can be referred to as "you". Pointing out that this contact is the cause of anxiety and why this is so, enables the patient to achieve, in the first instance, a distance from and an ability to think about the psychotic personality. This strengthens the nonpsychotic personality and eventually erodes the psychotic personality by a partial reintrojection of the split off, superego fragments. This is only possible if there is some healthy nonpsychotic personality.

I think that the tyrannical nature of the psychotic process suggests that it is comprised of minute reassembled fragments of a pathological, sadistic split off superego, as Bion suggested in "Cogitations" (1992, p. 31). This would account for its malignant, reality hating central core. O'Shaughnessy (1999) graphically describes the abnormal superego to abnormal superego transference which results in a therapeutic stalemate with escalation of hatred and anxiety and a dangerous situation with a possibility of psychotic breakdown.

The idea of working in a way that acknowledges psychotic and nonpsychotic personalities has been written about by Richards (1993), Sinason (1993) and Lucas (1998). All three authors underline the importance of working with an awareness of the divide between the psychotic and nonpsychotic personalities, which requires an ability to hold in mind the patient's and the therapist's psychotic and nonpsychotic personalities. They have developed a language in which this can be conveyed to the patient.

The idea of two or more personalities is embedded in the condition of Dissociative Identity Disorder (DID). Mollon (1999) talks of dissociation being a central feature of the psychotic process. However the countertransference "feel" of the psychotic process nonpsychotic personality divide, is different in DID and Schizophrenia and the clinical picture is different. Patients with a schizophrenic illness on the whole appear to function less well, have less intact affect, poorer emotional resonance and a greater narrowing of interests. Bion (1967), in "On Hallucination", may shed light on the matter when he describes how he conceives of the difference between splitting and dissociation.

Splitting, he says, is violent, is intended to produce minute fragmentation, and lines of demarcation which run counter to any natural lines of demarcation between one part of the psyche, or one function of the psyche and another. Dissociation is gentler, has respect for natural lines of demarcation between whole objects and indeed follows these lines to effect the separation. The patient suffering dissociation is capable of depression and betrays a dependence on the pre-existence of elementary verbal thought.

Bion uses splitting where he wishes to speak of developmental activity and dissociation to describe a benign process related to the nonpsychotic personality. This takes us further along the way to explain the tyrannical power of the psychotic process. Fairbairn (1981) and Grotstein (1994) developed their own theoretical models. Fairbairn (1981) has described an entrapping intrapsychic circle of communication, splitting of the mother into a good and a bad object which then resplit into a needed exciting object and a rejecting object. Grotstein (1994) reinterprets Fairbairn's structure. He believes that a "normal or particulate personality" has normal divisions and from time to time comes together as a "holographic personality" which is experienced as a subjective sense of whole-ness and at-one-ness.

The psychotic process attacks any lively external contact, including need of/anger towards/connection with external reality and in particular, contact with the therapist. Rather gentler dissociation occurs in the nonpsychotic personality which can experience, in the way most of us recognise, having two opposing thoughts about a matter—leading to the sort of internal dialogue with which most of us are familiar.

In the clinical example given (under heading "Psychotherapy for Psychosis?" Para 4) the patient Les (nonpsychotic personality) became the victim of ferocious attacks by the psychotic process Dob and was able to talk about them later. They were meted out because contact was made with the therapist during the initial assessment. The psychotic personality objects to being spoken about and revealed, presumably because that very process of relating indicates contact with external reality which is totally forbidden. For a while the patient Les was overwhelmed by the psychotic process Dob, on the verge of being readmitted to hospital and in danger of following the psychotic process' instructions to commit suicide "in order to stay safely and exclusively with Dob" (the psychotic process).

As a possible way of being able to empathise more readily with a patient overwhelmed by psychosis, I suggest the following. Imagine having made a huge gaffe which is enormously embarrassing. One might go home, have it rattle around in one's mind, intrude upon one's daily tasks, thoughts, conversations and wake one at 3 a.m. with ideas such as "why did I do it, I am such an idiot, X will be furious..." and so on. While enmeshed in such preoccupations one appears distracted in a dream-like way. A fairly well adjusted person would discuss it with friends who would say realistically reassuring things and a way would be found to repair the damage by an apology or explanation.

With a psychotic process, this inner triangle of attack on the vulnerable self and on the person who will retaliate, becomes a world war which is too dangerous to be allowed any contact with the rest of the psychic apparatus; hallucinations may also be experienced. The dialogue is elaborated using id and primary process content (delusions) and there is no reassurance or explanation capable of breaking into the dream-like, distracted state. It can take over and dominate the nonpsychotic part of the personality.

Clinical session

Madeleine, a patient in her 30s has been seen twice weekly for a number of years. Her biological mother, who had "nervous" problems left her in the care of a nursing home at birth. She was later adopted by an older couple who physically abused her. She was sexually abused for some years from the age of four. As a teenager she became a prostitute, took drugs for a brief period, shop lifted and killed several small animals in rather horrific ways. After her first baby she expressed homicidal and suicidal intentions. She was in and out of hospital for some years and developed classical first rank signs of a schizophrenic illness.

The first years of sessions became increasingly full of rage and acting out in the form of stomping out of sessions. The most violent, psychotic or depressed periods followed breaks which were felt by the patient to be indicative of the therapist/mother's hatred of and wish to get rid of the patient.

Apart from violent outbursts the sessions were and are mostly silent and heavy going. The therapist has to rely heavily on the countertransference as a guide to what is going on, whether the nonpsychotic or psychotic personality is present, the likelihood of acting out the violent impulses when taken over by the psychotic process and so on.

This session occurred approximately 18 months into the therapy and after a week's break. She had a name for her psychotic personality which has been present since her early teens which I shall call Fem.

The patient sat down looking glum. There was a silence in which there was a gradual change in the patient which the therapist picked up in the countertransference. She became more involved with something happening in her head.

The therapist, aware of this started by trying to gain access to her nonpsychotic personality. The next paragraph took place over about 10 minutes.

Therapist: You are having difficulty talking to me. I wonder what that is about? (Silence). It may have seemed a long time since the last session and that might make it difficult for you to speak to me. (Silence, angry sideways glance at therapist). I am noticing a change as you sit here. Is Fem around? (Silence). There is a lot of anger around in the room. What do you think that is about?
Patient: (Angrily) I have got nothing to say to you. (Her face was contorted with fury).
She got up looking furious and left the room. The therapist went after her. The patient flung her arms around threateningly as if to hit the therapist who was aware of feeling afraid.
Therapist: (In corridor) Come and sit down. I can see you are furious and you may be afraid. Try to speak to me about it.

After further negotiation she sat down.

Patient: YOU DON'T TALK TO ME. (She shouted).

The therapist, feeling angry, afraid and outraged made several attempts to open a dialogue suggesting that the patient might be feeling afraid, angry and outraged and that indeed the therapist had not been there to talk to her in between this and the last session. It was all to no avail and the therapist said eventually:

Therapist: Is Fem telling you to say that?

Patient: Noooo! (Said loudly with an upward inflection).

Therapist: It sound as if someone thinks I am accusing you of something.

Patient: (furiously) Nobody knows how ill I feel.

She went on to announce that she would complain that the therapist was harassing her—that she was not going to take her tablets—that she would not go to see her psychiatrist—that the therapist had refused to be her mother so she would not come back to therapy.

The therapist said that it appeared that the patient was very frightened, that the recent changes in her treatment had not made her any better and that she feared that the therapist would not be able to look after her properly, especially since there had just been a break. It might be frightening that the therapist saw her only twice a week and was not there in between the sessions.

There was a noticeable change in atmosphere. After a silence:-

Patient: (Out of the corner of her mouth in order to avoid being heard by Fem). Fem is telling me to do everything I can to make you get rid of me.

Therapist: Fem is telling you to push me away and provoke me into giving up on you.

Patient nodded.

Therapist: Is that what YOU want (addressing her nonpsychotic personality).

Patient: (quietly and sadly) No.

Therapist: No. I don't think that is what you want, and that is a good and healthy thing.

The session ended.

Two years later there are positive changes. The patient has had no admissions to hospital and only one minor crisis in the form of a suicide threat. Her husband reports that she is less impulsive. Her appearance has improved considerably. She has started doing tasks in the home. She is able to talk about how difficult she finds the breaks instead of being overwhelmed by the psychotic process. She is just beginning to experience guilt and the ability to reflect upon herself.

From the point of view of her quality of life, she believes things have improved. Her family are less stressed. It is also worth mentioning that despite the costs of regular twice weekly therapy, the financial cost of treatment is less than it would have been with multiple admissions and child care arrangements.

Conclusion

The potential for psychosis in man is universal. Exploiting this fact by an ever deepening knowledge of the primitive features within oneself is essential if one has to rely relatively heavily on countertransference for guidance in the therapeutic endeavour.

It is useful for psychotherapists to have a working knowledge of the biological aspects of psychosis. Amongst other advantages it helps to diminish therapeutic omnipotence!

A good assessment does not necessarily preclude the appearance of a psychotic illness at some stage during the psychotherapeutic process. "Mini" psychotic episodes in the form of transference psychosis or brief episodes of psychosis quite frequently occur in patients seen out of hospital environments.

In the model of psychosis presented, the psychotic process probably originates from a split off pathological superego which is split repeatedly with the most unendurable bits reassembled as tyrannical, attacking internal objects. These are attached to the relevant parts of the ego. This results in a circular, inward looking, self fuelled, self perpetuating and regenerating process. It is separated by an ever widening gulf from the nonpsychotic personality. Thus it is easy to see why the process should be experienced by the patient as something separate, possibly from outside and by the therapist as having totally different origins from the nonpsychotic personality.

In the consulting room early recognition of the psychotic process is important and not always easy. The change in transference in the move from the nonpsychotic to the psychotic process and the countertransference responses elicited are most helpful in the detection of the hidden psychotic process. Thus it is useful to know how to locate the psychotic personality and how to address the nonpsychotic personality.

CHAPTER TEN

Violence and hostility from a sense of unconscious shame: shame in the transference and countertransference

Simon Archer

> "I say that with those you love best you live in foulest shame unconsciously"
>
> Teiresias to Oedipus, "Oedipus The King"

This is David's account of his attempted murder of his wife:

"I knew what I had to do. It's what she wants. It's what we both want. My thoughts seemed to echo inside me, as if I was in a great empty chamber. Each word kept repeating itself like a slow, repetitive drum roll. Each thought seemed to be suspended in a great space. I felt that I was floating above myself, listening carefully to what I heard below me. I knew what I was doing, but my actions seemed to be those of a stranger. When I got up from my chair my movements seemed mechanical and precise. I unlocked the back door, and walked into the garden, across the wet grass to our summer house. My voice was ahead of me, pulling me along. I remember my movements so clearly now, over a decade later, that I find it difficult to understand why I could not then stop myself. I rummaged in the darkness until I found what I wanted: a large hammer, the sort used for banging fence stakes into the ground. Slowly, as though I was reliving a past experience in an unreal dream, I returned to the house, and trudged up the stairs, towards our bedroom. I knew what had to be done. It's what she wants, I kept thinking. I'm doing this for her sake; afterwards it will be my turn. I hit her several times with the hammer, until she woke, screaming". (Wigoder, 1987, p. 202).

David Wigoder was the pseudonym used by this patient of mine when he wrote the published account of this event some years afterwards. By then he had been in analytic therapy with me for nearly 2 years. He was an intelligent, distressed man who frequently found himself overwhelmed by unconscious forces. He seemed to have ideas about guilt but they were bland and lacking emotional content. David did not know why he had tried to kill his wife. While seeing him I had begun to take an interest in shame. I had encountered a number of adult psychotherapy patients who hovered on the margins of criminal activity. Also I was working with young, criminal offenders. Both of these groups seemed preoccupied with issues such as loyalty (rather than love), excommunication, shunning of enemies, concealment and losing face.

Defence or affect?

I will not attempt a comprehensive review of the literature on shame. Piers and Singer (1953), Miller (1985) and Nathanson (1987), among others, have done so and they include important contributions from authors not mentioned here. I have previously sketched (Archer, 1993) the way that ideas about shame shifted away from Freud's explanation of it as a "Dam against sexual excess" (Freud, 1905c, p. 191), that is, the defensive repression of a sexual-exhibitionistic drive.

It is not within the scope of this chapter to discuss the relationship between shame and the anal stage (e.g. Abraham, 1921). Shame is not a new thing arising out of this phase but comes sharply into focus at this time due to the intense emotions and fantasies genered around bowel control, the associated but now prohibited eroticism, and the increasing internal and external demand for socialisations.

We know what shame feels like. It is an unpleasant, acutely painful mental state of tension and discomfort. Our capacity to think and our integrity are temporarily shattered. We want to turn back the clock and undo the situation that has given rise to this painful state. We want to disappear or hide. It is these reactions that point to shame being not a defence, but a signal-anxiety that activates defences. Psychoanalytic writers following Freud (with Erikson, [1950] as a notable exception), usually wrote of "shame and guilt" without distinguishing the two. Although this is still often the case, shame is no longer the "Cinderella of the unpleasant emotions" (Rycroft, 1972, p. 152) that it was when he published his "Critical Dictionary". Cinderella has now left the kitchen hearth but is sometimes still found wandering without a properly established place in the psychoanalytic household.

Freud at times uses the terms ego-ideal and super-ego interchangeably (e.g. "The Ego and the Id", 1923a) and occasionally deals with them as if they are different concepts. Within the "Structural Theory", Freud (1914), saw the ego-ideal as linked with narcissism and as pre-oedipal in origin. Later, writing about the sense of inferiority, Freud linked it with the loving aspect of the parents: "A child feels inferior if he notices that he is not loved, and so does an adult" (1933 [1932], p. 65). The ego-ideal is the agency against which the individual evaluates his achievements. It is the internalised version of that which is held up by the *admiring, loving* parent as something for which to aim and it becomes the substitute for the lost, grandiose self-love of infancy. Freud links the sense of guilt with fear of the parents. The super-ego emerges out of the Oedipus complex when the feared, critical parent is internalised. The super-ego becomes the agency that measures the difference between the ego's actual achievement and the ego-ideal. In his lecture "Dissection of the Personality" (1933 [1932]) Freud attempts to tease apart the two mental states of inferiority and guilt. He says that, "Little attention has been given in psycho-analysis to the question of the delimitation of the two concepts" (p. 66). Feelings of inferiority and of shame are synonymous. Freud connects the sense of inferiority with a perceived lack of love, and seems to be thinking of feelings of inferiority as being an emotional response rather than a defence.

As early as 1893 Freud (p. 6) discusses shame as a traumatic affect that may activate defences. Erikson (1950) separated shame from guilt by proposing that shame arises out of conflicts within the pre-oedipal stage of "Shame versus Doubt and Autonomy", in which the child attempts to master feelings of helplessness. Other authors have pointed to other instances where Freud seems to be thinking of shame not as a defence but as a signal-anxiety indicating that the subject's self-image is threatened due to loss of approval, a sense of helplessness or vulnerability and negative self-valuation. Miller (1989) draws attention to Freud's idea of shame as a "feminine characteristic" and a defence against what he calls "genital deficiency", and to Freud's explanation of the Wolf Man's aggressive phantasies as an active compensation for his unconscious feeling of passive helplessness. In the case of the Wolf Man this gives rise to defensive, object-directed aggression which causes an overlay of guilt. Kinston (1983) suggests that in the "Interpretation of Dreams" where Freud (1900, p. 247) takes a dream of the unhappy wanderer to illustrate shame, Freud is putting shame (to quote Kinston), "beyond the pleasure principle", rather than equating it with the repression of a sexual drive. The wanderer is naked, exposed and wishes to hide. Kinston believes that Freud is describing the effect of narcissistic trauma in which the subject desires approval but experiences negative valuation. Erikson (1950), Chasseguet-Smirgel (1985a), Kinston (1982, 1983), Miller (1989), Mollon (1984), and Pines (1987), point to evidence that shame emerges as a key factor in pre-oedipal development, at a time when the infant struggles internally with narcissism, self-image, development of the ego-ideal and the recognition of the other.

Kinston describes the original stimulus for shame as an *inter*-psychic one, which is internalised as an *intra*-psychic object-relationship. He links the origin of excessive shame reactions and consequent defences, with on-going trauma caused by the impingement of narcissistically disturbed parenting upon the relatively helpless and immature infant psyche. There may be a repetition within the transference in the form of "passive-into-active" manoeuvres such as placating and the formation of temporary or permanent false-self moves or structures. Kinston regards these as a particular form of identification with the aggressor, the aggressor in this case being the narcissistically impinging parent who imputes negative value to the infant so that any positive achievement may be registered as negative. This situation explains the common experience that achievement or praise may, paradoxically, trigger shameful feelings. (A patient once said to me "when I am wrong I am wrong, and when I am right I am wrong").

Chasseguet-Smirgel (1985a) extends the concept of the ego-ideal. She redefines shame as an affect rather than as a defence, while retaining Freud's theoretical link with cathexis, libido and the drive theory. She describes the ego-ideal as the psychic agency that pulls the subject away from primary (grandiose) narcissism. It contains the idea of unconscious hope and of forward moving development engendered by the parental environment. We can deduce that in situations where there is a damaged, shame-driven parent, imbued with little hope, the child may need to reflect the parent's damaged ego-ideal and construct a fragile, false-self surface development with counterfeit oedipal identifications. There may be a strong underlying wish to return to primary narcissism, with accompanying hopelessness and unconscious shame. This was the internal situation of my patient David, whose damaged mother had eventually killed herself. The consequent construction of a negative ego-ideal will contribute to the formation of a severe super-ego.

Shame and guilt

A number of writers from different schools converge at the same point: shame is connected with self-image in a way that distinguishes it from guilt. Nathanson (1987, p. 5) puts it succinctly: "Wrongdoing may be punished by guilt; while unwarranted opinions about the self, when exposed, will be punished by shame ... guilt limits action, while shame limits narcissism". Chasseguet-Smirgel (1985a, p. 150) says "whereas guilt is aroused when a limit (established by the superego) is touched or transgressed, shame arises when a goal (set by the ego ideal) is not reached. Shame accompanies defeat, guilt transgression". Miller (1989, p. 238) states "Shame and guilt presumably are different experiences, with shame aroused when personal authority is minimal and guilt when it is used sadistically". Kinston (1983, p. 224) writes "it is an unpleasurable experience associated with the maintenance of narcissistic equilibrium". Mollon (1984, p. 208) says "Whereas in guilt we feel remorse in relation to something we have done in actuality or phantasy to another, shame concerns identity". For Pines (1987, p. 23) shame emerges in the mirror stage when "the child begins to recognise that he/she is now an object in a world of other objects, visible in a world of other visible persons, and that he/she can therefore be the object of the scrutiny of others in a disappointing or critical manner".

A wish for punishment indicates unconscious guilt. A wish to hide indicates unconscious shame. Defences against shame are manifestations of a wish to hide from oneself or from the seeing other. Depending on the pervasiveness of shame, an individual may use temporary manoeuvres against it, or may institute defences leading to permanent character pathology. These defences may range from temporary evasiveness to chronic impersonation and lying; from temporary dissociative states to persistent trance-like ones; from mild seductiveness to perversion; from false-self placatory behaviour to subversion (in which the seeing other is corrupted); from anger to murderous or suicidal rage (in which the seeing-other, or the seen-self is annihilated). Kinston defines such defensive manoeuvres as "object-narcissistic". Object-narcissism is a primitive object-relationship in which separateness is denied and in which "the object is destroyed and the emotional dependent needy part of the person is deprived of support and nourishment" (1982, p. 253). Shame signals that the subject's narcissistic equilibrium has been disturbed by the presence of an unconscious negative self-image. This prompts the individual to move away from too-painful self-scrutiny and merge into an object-narcissistic state with the therapist. Shame is then abolished, but at the cost of loss of autonomy. A move by a patient into a merged state with the therapist may, therefore, signal anxiety due to the presence of unconscious (or conscious but concealed) shame. A permanent move into a merged object-narcissistic state allows the subject to be *shameless*. This is the state in which feelings of shame are not allowed into consciousness. The person will feel then "in control" (of his objects), but at the cost of not feeling truly joined up with himself or with others in any meaningful way. This is a precarious state because the split-off negative self-images will permanently threaten the subject's equilibrium.

Biology: two theories

Nathanson (1987) summarises the work of Tomkins (1962, 1963). Tomkins (1995) proposes that detailed infant observation reveals the existence of several sets of affective responses which are signalled (as Darwin observed) by the face (and body) of the infant immediately or very soon after birth. The positive affects are: interest–excitement; enjoyment–joy; surprise–startle [sic]; The negative affects are: distress–anguish; anger–rage; fear–terror; shame–humiliation. These affect sets are a drive-independent biological system. The set designated by Tomkins as "shame–humiliation" is signalled by the baby turning away its face and by slumping its body. Nathanson and Tomkins cite a variety of observational researches showing the existence, from very early on, of this face/body shame reaction. An affect is without meaning and without content. The purpose of the affects is to provide a repertoire of responses to assist the survival of the infant whose brain must deal with a welter of incoming stimuli. Each of these affects has its own sub-cortical location that is triggered by the activation of a particular level and degree of stimuli within the brain. Proto-shame acts from infancy as an auxiliary to the positive affects. Nathanson summarises this by saying

> Tomkins postulates that the trigger to shame affect is any experience that requires rapid decrease in the affects of interest–excitement and enjoyment–joy in situations where the organism wishes to maintain the pre-existing affect state. Failure ranks high as such a trigger. [1987, p. 20]

Nathanson refers to observations of infants using proto-shame to reduce, or turn off the affect "interest–excitement" in a shiny object. Such responses have a survival purpose: The infant needs to be able to avoid becoming too interested in one single thing and needs to avoid its mental capacity being overwhelmed by stimuli. (Other levels or amounts of stimuli will trigger the other sets of affective responses.)

Within Tomkins' theory the shame-affect as displayed by the baby is *proto*-shame. It is an *affect*, not an emotion. The infant does not yet possess the cortical connections required to form such concepts as meaning. How does the affect proto-shame become the complex response of shame emotion? The relationship between each affect set and the rest of the brain rapidly evolves in complexity. For example, Nathanson proposes that Spitz's 8-month "stranger anxiety" can be seen as the infant making use of the shame response of turning away. "The infant decides to curtail communication because not everybody is mother, the primary mirror and communicant for his or her affective transmission". (1987, p. 7). With time a vast accretion of experiences will become associated with shame-affect. The mnemic traces of these experiences are activated whenever the shame response is triggered. What is originally a quantitative, physiological phenomenon to do with stimulus density evolves into a qualitative, psychological matter. The nature of the individual's particular psychical accretions around shame will determine whether or not shame is a bearable or catastrophic event. Shame-affect activates memories of other negative, shaming experiences that may, in turn, trigger the "location" for the innate biological affect set *anger/rage* by taking the brain over the continuous stimulus level for anger. This may cause yet further escalation because the brain location for anger–rage affect will have its own associated set of memories and phantasies. Therefore shame, which in one person might be a temporary disruption requiring temporary measures such as a passing wish to disappear might, in another, create a serious trauma causing major disintegration of the self requiring drastic defensive measures. For some individuals the possibility of the re-activation of this trauma is ever present as an ongoing, often nameless anxiety.

It remains to be seen if Tomkins' theory is correct. His ideas have an interesting congruence with some of Freud's speculations. The problem of how quantities of excitation become psychological qualities was something that preoccupied Freud (1938). Tomkins' proposal that any decrease in stimulus density activates the affect of enjoyment, (such as when hunger is reduced by eating) corresponds with Freud's pleasure/unpleasure principle in which the psyche strives to reduce unpleasurable tension caused by excessive stimuli. Tomkin's idea that a certain density of neural firings triggers each affect-location corresponds to the economic theory of "quantities of excitation".

Another researcher whose ideas I will refer to briefly is Gerald Edelman (1992, 1994). Edelman proposes that natural selection has created the brain as an organ of categorisation, recognition and learning, processes essential to survival. Edelman's central idea is that the brain is *not* like a computer, but is an almost unimaginably complex system of interconnected neurones and "maps" (locations where certain aspects of functioning are located within the brain), whose patterns of connection are unique for each individual. Each human is born with a brain that contains a huge "population" of potential neuronal connections. From (and before) birth this population evolves according to principles of Darwinian natural selection. Much of this population is never employed, but the vastness is required for the process of natural selection. An essential aspect of the theory is that patterns of neuronal firings within the cortex are reinforced or discarded (not reinforced), by electrochemical signals from the primitive (oldest) part of the brain, depending on whether or not this pattern has led to an action that has survival value. For example, initially, a baby's arm movements are absolutely random, but being able to touch an object has survival value. Any arm movement will have a corresponding pattern and sequence of neuronal synapse firings. When the baby touches something, that particular sequence of firings will be reinforced by the primitive brain, which gives "value" to touching objects. Edelman's theory is elegant and compelling. He has much to say about memory and consciousness that could be of interest to psychoanalysis. He thinks, like Tomkins, that innate inhibitory processes are used to curtail mental activities such as attention. Edelman and Tomkins provide biological models for the sense of achievement. The inherent positive "value"; given to developmental achievement (such as touching and focussing on objects) could be thought of as a biological basis for the concept of the ego-ideal as a forward driving, progressive force. It is possible to think of Tomkins' affect set of enjoyment–joy as slowly accreting to itself more and more positive experiences of joyous achievement. If, on the other hand, we think of an infant experiencing this positive valuation imparted by the primitive part of the evolving brain, or the affect enjoyment–joy being constantly contradicted by a severely prohibitive or inhibiting parent, we might then expect to find the sort of confusion, inhibition and identity disturbance experienced by shame-driven patients.

To return to David:

He was able to identify several incidents throughout his life that had triggered acute shame, propelling him into sudden action that had made him want to flee, hide or kill himself. For example, while working excessive hours (in order to gain approval) from an employer who had become a friend, he had said, one day, that he needed to leave at 5 p.m. His employer told him to go home and be with his family but added a humorous aside about the "English not working the way we do". This pitched David into a drastic state of shame. Feeling enraged he fled to the U.S.A. and hid. David was well camouflaged and at first I could only guess at what was underneath this surface. Many hours of psychotherapy revealed that before he had attacked his wife he had been overwhelmed by unbearable shame. In a manic phase he had embezzled a huge sum of money from his employers' account. They fired him, kept the matter quiet and arranged for him to repay the money. He obtained (by charm) another highly paid job but his bank manager, who had learned of the embezzlement, was also, by chance, his new employer's bank manager. He told David that he would block any finance for David's new employer if David were to be involved. He advised David to leave the area and change his name. David had yet to tell his wife, who already knew about the embezzlement and his being fired. This is what David wrote about the events immediately preceding the attack:

> Helen looked pale. At 6.30, after Vanessa [his daughter] had gone to bed, Helen, holding a bottle of tranquillisers, said: "I'm going to bed. I wish I could go to sleep, and never wake up." And that, I thought, as she left the room, is before she's heard my ruinous news ... Ben, then 7 years old, kept me company until he was too tired to stay awake. By 11 o'clock I was alone, sitting in my study. I probably sat there for an hour or so, listening to the voices screaming inside my head. There's nothing more I can do! I can't go on! I've had enough! She's had enough! She wants to be dead! So do I! [Wigoder, p. 201]

David was evasive and seemed to know this. His childhood experience had been of a demanding, narcissistically disturbed mother who pretended to care about him but who was, he felt, ultimately concerned only with her own suffering. Throughout his childhood, whenever he experienced any strong emotion that contradicted his mother's need for constant approval, she would attack him relentlessly. Her final selfish act, as David saw it, was her suicide (when he was 35). David had made more than one suicide attempt. He seemed occupied with the image that he presented to the world. In the therapy he put pressure on me to accept the competent version of himself that he presented to me and would, unconsciously, use any means at his disposal, such as humour, seduction or coercion, to maintain that image. I knew David used charm with me and he was frank about his ability to charm others.

When David told me of his attack on his wife, I heard his words as the manifest content of his story. What was the latent content? His wife had said that she did not want to wake up. He eventually knew that in thinking "She's had enough" he had believed his wife was saying he was useless, and that she had seen through him. When connected with his past, it became clear that this was a disaster that repeated an ever-present internal situation in which he was forever fending off shame, seeing himself as lacking, inferior or wrong. (*Not* bad and guilty but *wrong and ashamed*). Like a dream, his written account is condensed but there are some clues pointing to shame as a determining factor. There is the sense of dissociation from himself, the wish to rid himself of the other who sees him as he really is; the reactive, compulsive act of violence that is linked to "reliving a past experience" and the experience of himself as mechanical or robotic. (Kinston [1983] describes the defences against the emergence of shame that lead to the robotic, de-humanising of the self and others.) David had married a woman who represented an idealised, admiring object with which he was fused. He needed this narcissistic object to reflect back to him his idealised image of himself. (This idealised, grandiose self may have been unconsciously reflected in his choice of his unusual nom de plume, "Wigoder" with its second syllable "god".) When this broke down he was suddenly faced with a true image of himself: unable to connect with her and able only to counterfeit love. When she no longer complied with his unconscious demand for absolute approval, his identity was acutely threatened and she had to be eliminated. After a long period of therapy David was able to begin to live more comfortably with his shame. Only then was he able to think about real, rather than counterfeit guilt and begin to repair his damaged internal and external relationships.

Shame and countertransference

I am now going to use another patient "John" to further illustrate some of the problems and characteristics of a group of patients in whom shame is a significant determining factor.

In our consultation "John" told me he had an insoluble problem. He had to choose between two women. There was a pattern of his falling in love with a woman other than his current partner. He would use charm to keep the two women on a string but when he was with one he would always want to be with the other. He wanted me to tell him how to make the choice. I began to feel bored as he told me his story in a rehearsed, relentless way. I needed to force myself to pay attention as my mind wandered off. I began to feel incompetent and rather ashamed. I registered these feelings and continued to struggle with them. Suddenly I woke up as he seemed to deliver a message "out of the blue" not connected with anything else he was saying, right from his unconscious: "I never run for a bus you know, I would look such an idiot". I thought about my feeling of shame and said that I wondered if he was telling me about very difficult feelings of inferiority. This allowed him to talk about how he felt constantly on the alert for anything that would make him feel exposed and ashamed. He said that he would often, when with woman "A", find himself thinking disturbing thoughts such as "if she really knew what I was like she wouldn't want to be with me". These thoughts would make him run to woman "B", in an attempt to avoid a shameful negative self-image. He would then feel better for a while but the whole process would begin again, as woman "B" became, in turn, the frightening, disapproving other who must be eliminated from his life and from his mind. John told me that his mother had cared for him in a conditional way. She had been arbitrary, demanding, self-centred and frequently verbally cruel. She would approve of him only if he was good and made her feel good. Otherwise she would threaten him with disapproval. This meant that certain feelings, such as anger, were not acceptable. Any need that he might express was countered by his mother implying that her need and suffering were far greater. John thought (as did David) that his weak father always placated his mother.

John brought groups of dreams. The first dream would have little or no anxiety and be based around an apparently ordinary event. It would be difficult to find any latent content. The second dream would illustrate a sense of regressing. For example he would dream that he was literally, anxiously sliding downhill. The third dream would be the most disturbing. He would, for example, dream of arriving at my consulting room to find me looking decrepit, dirty and dishevelled. This would make him angry. Why was he seeing such a useless, filthy incompetent therapist? This pattern of dreaming seemed best understood as being an expression of his denied, shameful self-image being projected onto me. The first "bland" dream in the sequence I understood as a camouflaged version of the final dream. Sometimes the third dream, which would leave him depressed, would contain acts of violence perpetrated by him. I saw this dream-violence as his way of trying to destroy the shaming other, often obviously the therapist.

John coped with what he experienced as the humiliation of needing help from me by imagining that he was superior to me. At first he could not think of us as in any way equal. He needed to look down on me. He would try to humiliate me by making me react sadistically so that he could tell himself that after all I was the "bastard" he found himself calling me when he was away from me. Frequently he would succeed in making me feel useless and hopeless about him. This would make him want to rid himself of me by stopping the therapy. This kind of situation can easily become destructive in that the therapist's own narcissistic equilibrium may be disturbed. In these circumstances, if the underlying shame, due to negative-self evaluation is not attended to, the therapist, whose interpretations may be felt as diminishing "attacks", may inadvertently cause the patient to react defensively, with hostility. Many of the defensive phenomena I referred to above may occur in the transference situation and may find a corresponding response in the therapist who may become stupefied or sleepy or be made to laugh inappropriately, be excited, feel seduced, made a fool of or excommunicated. These countertransference responses are likely to make the therapist, who may feel disturbed, fend off impending shame by means of retaliatory silence, or elegant but critical or sadistic interpretations. The way that the therapist deals with this projected shame may be crucial to the outcome of the therapy. The situation may become an intractable "shame–guilt cycle" (Mollon, 1984) in which there is a repetition-compulsion, without insight, of an unconscious sado–masochistic relationship in the transference and countertransference. The patient avoids shame, due to a sense of passivity and help-lessness, by means of active, destructive, defensive attacks upon the therapist as one-who-sees and disapproves. This causes *secondary* guilt, fear of retribution and further reinforcement of helplessness and negative self-mages, leading to further shame and so on. In these cycles, two separate, but inter-locking lines of development of shame and guilt interact. It is important to try to separate them, otherwise the patient will feel increasingly distressed and persecuted by escalating shame and guilt. This distress will be compounded by interpretations about hostility that do not take into account its cause.

Sometimes John would slide into a sleepy trance in which he was inaccessible and I felt cut off from him. I would find the same thing happening to me. Sometimes whole sessions would pass in this way leaving me feeling incompetent. This would lead to John complaining that I was useless and he would become angry and distressed. John managed shame by unconsciously aiming to provoke me into failure in this and other ways. This unconscious wish to shame the therapist is driven by the patient's need to rid himself of painful, negative self-images, to do with a shameful sense of ruthlessness. When I was able to interpret this projective process John began to be able to monitor his state of mind. He became able to identify the triggers for his trance-like state so that he could stop them. He became able to own the shameful idea that he did not know how to love another person because he could only (like his internalised mother) think about his own needs. Eventually John was able to have conscious fantasies about attacking me of a more oedipal sort, which he could even enjoy without too much guilt, rather than repressing them and unconsciously dramatising them in the transference. He was anxious when he suddenly imagined beating me up but was relieved when he could see that I did not react as if his fantasy was the same as his actually doing it. Finally he began to find a sense of real concern for me as a separate individual.

Sexuality and shame

Affects, as theorised by Tomkins, are a biological system separate from the drives, but any of the affect sets can become suffused with any of the drives. (For example, a person's shame-affect may become so associated with negative phantasies about eating and hunger that anorexia may result.) Chasseguet-Smirgel, writing from a more classical viewpoint retains Freud's connection between the ego-ideal, sexuality and exhibitionism. The ego-ideal is a positive force that pushes the individual forward, out of infantile sexuality and perversion. Because we have a tendency to hide from our ego that which is contradictory to the ego-ideal, "we fear being seen by our peers in situations that are narcissistically unsatisfactory" (1985a, p. 151). The unconscious ego-ideal pushes development ahead through infantile "perverse" sexuality, including homosexual identification with the same gender parent. Usually this homosexual libido is desexualised and displaced onto ordinary social relationships. The approval that we seek is exhibitionistic:

> the wish to receive narcissistic confirmation from one's peers (to diminish the margin between the ego and the ideal) leads the subject to exhibit himself to them. If this exhibition fails to ensure such satisfaction (if a narcissistic injury or a "social humiliation" results), the re-sexualisation of homosexuality renders the narcissistic injury equivalent to castration. [1985a, p. 161]

In Chasseguet-Smirgel's view, it is the re-sexualisation of previously sublimated infantile sexuality, as a result of narcissistic injury that causes a chain reaction: loss of approval → narcissistic wound →

collapse of the ego-ideal → re-emergence of "bound" homosexuality → castration-anxiety → shame. Whatever the sequence of cause and effect, shame and sexuality are closely associated.

John was acutely self-conscious about all aspects of his body and his sexuality. In attempting to deal with impending shame John would frequently exercise obsessively to build his muscles and would then admire himself in a full-length mirror. Occasionally his heterosexual identity would break down and he would be overtaken with homosexual feelings, which would leave him confused and ashamed. Sometimes this would emerge in the transference when he would be overtaken by anxiety that he or I was homosexual. This could suddenly lead to him picturing himself attacking and anally raping me in order to humiliate me and render me helpless. These fantasies alarmed the patient and puzzled me until I was able to understand them as provoked by his feeling overwhelmed by shame and rage, due to his idea that I had a negative opinion about him.

When shame is used to moderate narcissism, it is a maturing experience essential to loving and civilised relationships. After the initial pain of shame, the individual recovers and realises others have seen him as he knows he truly is, and not how he would merely wish to be seen. He may then be able to make use of shame as a force for change rather than treat it as an enemy to be annihilated. When shame is avoided, pathological narcissism, counterfeit behaviour, hostility or violence may result. With David, John and similar patients, a major part of the analytic task is to uncover concealed or denied shame. Shame has begun to find a place within psychoanalytic thinking. There have been attempts, some more satisfactory than others, to incorporate it into existing theory. There are also ideas from outside psychoanalysis about the origins of shame that are worthy of our attention. Shame undoubtedly plays a part in many, if not all, psychological disturbances and may be *the* most important factor in some. In the analytic consulting room countertransference shame can play a crucial part in understanding patients. Thinking about our shame may, in itself, trigger shame-affect. Perhaps this has made it a relatively neglected subject.

CHAPTER ELEVEN

The suicidal patient

A. H. Brafman

M ichael Balint was the supervisor for my first analytic training case. He was then an old man and we all knew that he had started practising when very young. Besides being an eminent member of the analytic society, Balint was deeply involved in applying psychoanalytic knowledge to general practice and in various experiments with different models of psychotherapy. This meant that his clinical experience was quite phenomenal. One day, I came for my session very shaken after the news of the suicide of a colleague. We talked about this and I ended up asking Balint how he dealt with suicidal patients. He burst out laughing, a striking, very characteristic laugh and, quite gently, told me "I have never taken on suicidal patients!" I did not quite believe him, but he refused to change his answer or to reveal to me the clues that might help me to recognize such patients.

Identifying a suicidal patient is not as easy as lay people might imagine it to be. There is the old myth that those who talk about it will not do it, even though when it does occur there will be plenty of people pointing a finger and saying we should have heeded the patient's warnings. Then it is a simple and obvious fact that it makes a difference when "suicide" is either the subject of phantasies and might involve impulses referring to intentions, i.e. part of the future, or that painful situation when it has become a known fact. A further, very subtle complication involves the complex range of thoughts, words and behaviours that can be included under the heading of "suicidal". Ordinary medical jargon will refer to a patient having "attempted suicide" or made a "suicidal gesture". This differentiation arises from an assessment of the degree of danger incurred by the patient in the attempt against his life, but I see a derogatory implication in it. Does our psychoanalytical classification of "suicidal" help us better to evaluate the risks presented by any one particular patient?

Ordinary psychotherapeutic practice does not often give us the opportunity of speaking to a patient who attempted suicide during or soon after the actual crisis. Work in a hospital casualty department presents too many such opportunities and it is very striking to find that virtually each patient has his own definition of what his behaviour was meant to achieve. "I couldn't take any more", "I felt I just had enough", "There was nothing left to look forward to", "I have no idea, I just know that I could not carry on any longer", are some common phrases. If we inquire further about the patient's feelings before the attempt on his life, we learn that beyond these expressions of despair and hopelessness there was also anger, hatred, bitterness and a wide range of affects not only about himself but also about relevant people in his life. But a more elusive distinction can be found in each one of these patients: what kind of death were they aiming to achieve? However absurd this question may appear, closer inquiry will show us that each person has his own notion of *what death means*.

In my experience as a clinician and as a teacher I have found that each person's concept of *death* and *suicide* is highly dependent on his own life experiences. Surprising as it might seem, it is not rare to find trainees who can expand at length over the theoretical formulations underlying these events, while lacking any personal direct experience of them.

A 10-year-old child died in a crisis of *status asthmaticus*. He had been in three times per week psychotherapy for the previous 2 years. When the clinical team discussed this tragic outcome, it emerged that the therapist knew he had asthma and had worked with him as having a "psychosomatic pathology", but she had never thought that death was a possibility to be considered.

In our psychoanalytic literature on suicidal ideation and behaviour, most formulations stem from three basic premises: (1) adult behaviour is influenced, if not determined, by early experiences; (2) the psychic mechanisms of introjection and projection lead to the unconscious experience of the self and of parts of the body as representations of relevant objects; and (3) aggressive impulses are part of our inborn instinctual endowment.

In his 1915 paper on "Mourning and melancholia", Freud discussed a person's reaction to the loss of a significant other. The identification with the lost object leads to the originally object-directed affects being turned against the self.

> The analysis of melancholia now shows that the ego can kill itself only if... it can treat itself as an object—if it is able to direct against itself the hostility which represents the ego's original reaction to objects in the external world. [p. 252]

Eglé Laufer discussed suicide in adolescence and she summarizes her views:

> Suicide is a violent action directed at the person's own body. This action is motivated by a fantasy and as such is defined as a break with reality which constitutes a psychotic episode. ... The fact that suicide attempts in young people almost always first occur after puberty has been reached [helps us to see] the meaning of the suicidal act as a violent attack on the adolescent's new sexual body. [1987, p. 1]

Campbell (1999, p. 76) describes how the body is experienced by the suicidal person as "an object concretely identified with the lost loved and hated person... in these patients a split in the ego has resulted in a critical and punitive superego perceiving the body as a separate, bad or dangerous object." He emphasizes the role of an unconscious phantasy that considers the attack on the body as a solution to the experience of loss.

These authors stress the person's inability to utilize reality testing to recognize what is self and what is other, as well as the incapacity to distinguish between the whole of the self and a body part of that self. It is important to bear these hypotheses in mind, since most patients will refer to their suicidal wishes and to any past suicidal behaviour in the language of everyday shared logic. Only the formulation of the appropriate questions will elicit the answers that will allow us to understand the unconscious experience of that particular patient. It will always surprise the patient suddenly to discover that just before and during the suicidal act there was a suspension of that reality testing he professes to be able to sustain: which is why Laufer brings in the word "psychotic". It is only if the patient can acknowledge the plausibility of this discovery that analytic work can hope to bring some insight to him.

These shifts from rational thinking to irrational experiencing in suicidal patients create subtle paradoxes. The briefest and most accurate formulation of these is given in an illuminating article on suicide by Maltsberger and Buie (1980, p. 71): "It is the paradox of suicide that the victim, finding inner death in life, seeks inner life in death." How true and helpful this sentence is, can be seen when discussing suicidal acts with the patient. It is surprisingly common to find a patient expressing his idea that successful suicide might mark the beginning of a happier life: but this is usually said with a belief (or conviction) that it is no more than a turn of phrase.

It is important to note the link made in psychoanalytic literature between suicide and violence (see, e.g. Perelberg, 1999). This follows Freud's instinct theory and results in considering aggressive phantasies, impulses and actual behaviour as part of the same continuum. From a theoretical perspective this formulation appears attractive and convincing. At the risk of being over-simplistic, these theoretical formulations mean that: (a) "aggression" encompasses the whole range of behaviours from, e.g., self-cutting, to murder or suicide; and (b) that there can be a blurring of the distinction between self-directed attack to an attack on an other (see, however, Glasser, 1985). However, in clinical practice it is quite imperative to assess the patient's use of language, his ability to distinguish between phantasy and reality and, above all, his capacity for impulse control. These are not easy features to assess in a consultation and even in the context of a long-term therapy, oscillations may occur and the therapist must be alert to keep under constant review his diagnostic evaluation of the patient's actual and potential abilities in these areas.

Campbell (1999, pp. 76–77) discusses his finding that his suicidal patients presented a recurring picture of their psychopathology: "a mothering object who was perceived as dangerous and untrustworthy". Even if he found different types of suicidal phantasies, each one "was underpinned by a wish for the "surviving self" to merge with an idealised maternal imago". Maltsberger and Buie (1980, p. 71) confirm the same constellation, referring to a "quest of rebirth into the arms of a comfort-giving mother". These authors also underline the significance of the father in the histories of these patients: he is seen as an absent figure who failed to intervene into that image of near-fusion between infant and mother, leading to distorted Oedipal configurations. Laufer (1987), in her discussion of adolescent suicide, prefers to stress the patient's self-image, self-esteem and feelings about his/her body and how each of these affects and is affected by his/her awareness of the relationship with each parent. I think that however useful these formulations are for an understanding of suicidal behaviour, they can be equally found in many other patients who present totally different clinical pictures and may never turn to destructive behaviour.

I believe that people nowadays take far greater life-threatening risks than in previous decades. Death by bondage has a long history, but unprotected sex in a casual sexual encounter is a new version of an old danger. Not everybody will agree that smoking is an attempt at shortening life, but taking ecstasy or other tablets supplied by a stranger is now a serious risk. Self-cutting has long been known, but at which point does this turn into life-threatening behaviour? Binge-eating or starvation diets are part of history, but when do they become suicidal-equivalents? Youngsters have formed gangs and adults have joined clubs, but when do we decide that our patient has moved from a wish to feel part of a group to offering himself as a sacrificial lamb? Do we ever see in our consulting rooms the new brand of believer who decides that suicide makes him a worthy martyr? Probably not, but how do we decide when adherence to a religious or political faith puts the patient's life in danger? (If this sounds too absurd, we have an example in pregnant women advised to abort a pregnancy for serious medical reasons, who refuse to do this out of their religious view of the meaning of pregnancy).

I think these facts of the patient's life are extremely important to take into account. However relevant our reconstructions of the patient's early relationships, his present life circumstances must never be minimized, let alone ignored. For many years now there has been a growing obsession with the idea that only "transference interpretations of the here and now" constitute valid therapeutic interventions. Unfortunately, much too often "transference" is seen as the therapist representing the embodiment of the patient's earliest objects and this tends to blind the therapist to the actual events of the patient's present life. If the patient takes large amounts of alcohol and drug cocktails at weekends, it may be a correct interpretation of the patient's deeper unconscious levels to speak about his need to gain control over a poisoning, punishing breast, as a denial and a defence against the analyst's absence. But what of the analyst's feeling of horror and impending disaster? How to decide whether this is a legitimate countertransference response, or the result of the analyst's prejudices and/or personal anxieties? At which point does unorthodox behaviour become life threatening? And when are we entitled to consider this "suicidal"? These are difficult decisions, but they must be faced. Once we are convinced that the patient is suicidal or represents a danger to others, we must also decide whether it is correct to continue analysis as before or whether there are new conditions calling for some departure from the usual interpretative technique.

In my experience, whatever might have been their early experiences, the worst problem experienced by suicidal patients is their isolation. Thinking of the ordinary person who attempts or commits suicide, discovering how isolated they were from family, friends, neighbours, any people in fact, tends to be a very common post-facto finding. But when suicidal thoughts or behaviour appear in a patient under therapy, it may be difficult for the therapist to recognize, let alone to deal with, that patient's isolation. One common example may be quoted: the patient who demonstrates that his therapy sessions have become the sum total of his life interests. A therapist who concentrates exclusively on the analysis of the "transference in the here and now", will interpret this patient's feelings as resulting from his dependence on the analyst-early mother figure. However "correct" this may appear, he may lose sight of the patient's possible sense of isolation and not appreciate how catastrophic it might be for the patient to have nobody else to turn to when the analyst, for whatever reason, is not available. I am not advocating that the therapist should summon a social worker to make the patient engage in social gatherings. I am, rather, concerned that the therapist may fail to spot those situations where the patient feels that suicide is the only way of dealing with the absence of the therapist, since his sessions have become the whole *raison d'être* of his life.

Case 1

A woman in her late 30s sought therapy because she was, once again, finding herself in an unsatisfactory relationship. She was very successful in her career and her partner was a senior member of staff in a related company. They loved each other, but she complained that he was constantly denigrating her and mocking her efforts at work and in their social life; when drunk, he would repeatedly voice how much he loved her, but when sober he was distant and superior. Their sexual life had been satisfactory for some time, but now he would occasionally tease her, asking if she "wanted to be serviced", a phrase she found offensive and very hurtful.

She had seen an analyst in the past, but she now became very attached to me. She wrote letters and, clearly, continued her sessions long after leaving me. She reported gaining in confidence and this led her to challenge her partner to change his behaviour. At one point, she reported with enthusiasm meeting another man and this brought up the hope of discovering a new life. Sadly, there was disappointment and one day I was unexpectedly called by her partner, who told me that she had committed suicide. There had been a previous suicidal attempt, not long before she had come to see me, but I had to admit being taken by surprise at the news of her death.

Checking my notes, I could see that this young woman had felt let down by the three men on whom she had pinned her hopes. There had been a period when she pleaded I should give her more of myself, but I could not see how I could possibly meet such a hope. What most impressed me was the fact that, even though my patient always mentioned endless names of people with whom she was involved at and through work, there was not really a single person with whom she might share her feelings of despair at her failure to find a man who would give her the children she had wanted for many years.

Going through her history, I could find many references to how she had experienced frustrations and disillusionment from her parents. Nevertheless, the only datum that I thought was convincingly significant referred to a younger sister who had been born prematurely, with a severe mental handicap. This girl had lived for years in institutions and my patient had grown up under severe orders never to make any reference to anyone about the existence of this sister. I have found other cases where this experience has led a patient to feel that he/she is not entitled to enjoy his/her being alive, as if their life had been gained at the expense of the existence of a sibling.

I might hypothesize that I should have seen the patient for more sessions each week (she had turned this down), but I do not believe this would have prevented her suicide. This was a patient who travelled often to other countries, from where she might write me letters, which underlined her dependence on my being available to her. In spite of this, I was left with the impression that her suicide was related to her conscious awareness of being stuck in an unsatisfactory relationship with no hope of becoming pregnant. It is a tempting speculation to imagine that she wanted to bring to life her handicapped sister and give her a better chance of life, but approaching the end of her 30s introduced a sense of pressure and despair which the patient found unbearable.

Case 2

This was a young man aged 23, who "wanted to know" himself better. His father was in his 50s when my patient was born. A most distinguished figure in his professional field, he died when the patient was 15. He was described as an enormous, gauche, dictatorial man, who "wanted to be loving, but just couldn't".

Mother was in her early 40s when the patient was born, "she just squeezed me in!". She was dominated by her husband, always complained of an unhappy life and now drank to excess. There was a sibling, already in mid-adolescence when my patient was born and, when he was 3 years old, a child of 10 died in an accident. He recounted how his mother kept photos of her children, but none depicted them beyond the age when the middle one had died. A further statement of his feelings regarding how his parents saw him, was "my parents always wanted more children, but could not afford it, so only when they got some money were they able to have me". "I was a half-replacement child". "Don't misunderstand me—I'm very happy that I'm here! But I still feel that perhaps they ought not to have had me!"

He was always punctual for his sessions and seemed to feel that they helped him to decide how to plan his future. He had been an enormously successful student, even though he had hated his years at boarding school. He tried to keep away from his mother, finding it difficult to accept her excessive drinking, and had virtually no contact with his older sibling. He had inherited money and managed to keep a good relationship with the man appointed as his trustee. Sessions were always lively and he had a rich social life. Names of friends and acquaintances, male and female, were put forward by the dozen. But as the months passed, his occasional experiments with cannabis snowballed into the more and more frequent use of cocaine: he claimed this was used by all members of his circle.

When he told me one day that he had allowed a person he had just met to inject him with some drug, I became quite worried. I interpreted his wish to belong and be accepted, his wish to find some direction out of his indecision about the future and other conflicts we had discussed before. As time went on, drug dealers came on to the scene and I was convinced my patient's wealth had become an essential attraction to his friends and to others that just came into his life.

A crisis occurred when he found himself knocked out by some drug cocktail he had thought was safe. When he mentioned fears of men who wanted to attack him and who claimed he was holding on to drugs and money that was theirs, it was quite impossible to decide whether this was fact or paranoid anxiety. But as long as he attended his sessions or telephoned to explain an absence, I managed to keep my own anxiety in check. He could agree with me that he was now playing a kind of Russian roulette, but he still insisted I was "getting it all out of proportion". And the predictable (at least in hindsight!) day came when he spent most of the session speaking of his terror of being attacked, then failing to turn up for the following session.

After telephoning his house and getting no reply for several times, I considered what to do and ended up calling the police. I explained my anxiety and requested they checked whether the patient needed help. The police gained access to my patient's flat and found him totally knocked out, but alive, claiming he could look after himself. The following day one of my patient's friends delivered a letter to my house, where he explained he could no longer have confidence in me and was, therefore, terminating the analysis. I tried, without success, to speak to him on the telephone and then wrote a letter explaining why I had decided to take the action I had taken. I had no proper reply, only a cheque in payment for due sessions.

Barely a fortnight later, the patient's sibling called me to inform me that the brother had been found dead, apparently from an "accidental drug overdose". I was left with the doubt whether this had been truly accidental, deliberately self-inflicted or some form of murder. I also had to contain my impulse to contact the police again and alert them to what was going on in my patient's social circle.

There is no doubt that my patient's early life was significant in influencing his incapacity to gather the fruits of his academic success. I give great importance to his sense of never having been a welcome son, feeling both parents as distant, though each for different reasons. But, on balance, I do consider most important the development where my patient became totally engulfed by the world of drugs. To the best of my knowledge, as recounted by the patient, every single one of his friends was completely absorbed by use of drugs, which left him with no access to anyone who could exert some counter-balancing influence on him.

Discussion

I have no desire to belittle the importance of a person's early life in shaping his future. Working with children and their parents (Brafman, 1997, 2001) I have found convincing evidence to show how their interactions can shape the development of the individual. But, equally important, this work has shown me how little one can extrapolate from findings in childhood to predict the subsequent development of each child. Indeed, focusing on the adult it is perfectly possible, if not plainly easy, to construct hypotheses linking early features of his/her past with the present day features of that person's life.

I think it is very salutary to remember that those patients we see are a minimal percentage of similar individuals in the community that never come under our scrutiny. It is legitimate and inevitable that we build our theories on our clinical experience, but we must still take into account the significance of the fact that our patient comes to see us. However "destructive" and "hostile" we may consider him to be, we must explain his attendance and his willingness to pay us our fees. Even if the patient is part of a research project and pays no fees, there must still be a good part of his self determined to make the effort to attend. If it is possible that there is some re-enactment in the transference of a sado–masochistic, destructive relationship, the patient must be holding on to some hope that this is only part of his total self.

Along similar lines, I also think there is a difference between a patient who *acts* violently and another who phantasizes about such attacks. Predictably, both kinds of patients arouse powerful feelings in the therapist, but any understanding of the countertransference demands the recognition of which of these groups the patient belongs to. Analysts and therapists do think of themselves as immune to destructive behaviour and this only reinforces the need to examine very carefully our reaction to a patient who has become so aware of his capacity for violence and damage, that he has sought professional help. Indeed, our empathy can lead to identification with the patient's unconscious self and object representations (Sandler, 1976), but these must be carefully disentangled from emotional reactions originating in our own sentiments about the patient, his behaviour and the world he reports in the sessions.

Perhaps I could finish by returning to Balint's joke. The price we pay as trainees or as part of the beginning of our clinical practice is that we consider ourselves lucky to *have* a patient. During training they are sent to us after a selection process and during early stages of practice we do not dare to choose which patients to work with: we are under pressure not to question or antagonize the referrer, in case we jeopardize further referrals. But as time goes on, we owe it to ourselves to establish what kind of patients we feel comfortable enough to work with. In other words, we must learn under what conditions we can work at our best. The kind of patients discussed in the present paper represent a group of patients that test to an enormous limit the therapist's capacity to retain his thinking abilities intact. From this point of view, it makes no difference whether we take on a patient just recovering from a serious suicidal attempt or another patient who is cutting her arms or still another patient who is drinking to excess. Whatever diagnostic assessment we reach about the patient's pathology, it is important to consult our knowledge of our limits. I believe this is what Balint tried to teach me—at least, this is the lesson I have learned.

CHAPTER TWELVE

Separation anxiety in relation to breaks in therapy

Helen Alfillé

"Out of tears, thoughts"

Leon Wieseltier, Kaddish

I was intrigued to watch a 14-month old toddler playing recently. It was the familiar game of peep-bo, making his father disappear by shutting the door, chuckling when father reappeared. Then the door really shut and the baby could not open it. The anxiety was palpable; the object was no longer under his control and father was gone. Two days later the game was repeated and the baby understood not to slam the door shut; this time the object was satisfactorily under control and always reappeared. As this game, in its many forms, is repeated endlessly, the little boy begins to sort out many mysteries. As Freud says:

> It (the infant) cannot as yet distinguish between temporary absence and permanent loss. As soon as it loses sight of its mother it behaves as if it were never going to see her again; and repeated consoling experiences to the contrary are necessary before it learns that her disappearance is usually followed by her re-appearance. [1926, p. 169]

I believe too that the 14-month old toddler was demonstrating the continuous process of differentiation and the gradual creation of an image of the object in his mind; he opens the door and there *is* daddy and eventually he trusts that his father will be there. The creation of the internal object has started. For the toddler quoted above, the game also involved control—he decided when to see his father and when to expel him; he had understood that the internalised object can be both present and absent.

In contrast to the above observation, I watched a 2-year old playing happily on his own for some time. He was concentrating on one toy and then moving to another, continually referring back to his mother either by glance or demand to "look Mummy"; he was replenishing both his external and internal worlds with the external object. If his mother left the room, the play effectively stopped as he somewhat anxiously awaited her return. As he develops trust, he will replenish himself with his internal object.

> In the course of time the individual introjects the ego-supportive mother and in this way becomes able to be alone without frequent reference to the mother or mother symbol. [Winnicott, 1958, p. 32]

With the little boy quoted, his partly internalised benevolent mother gave him the freedom to be creative in his play. But if she left the room, his anxiety led to a need to replenish in Mahler's sense of emotional or libidinal refuelling. And, after all, his mother is not an entirely loved object; she is also the frustrating mother who arbitrarily leaves him to go out into her own world. A balance is needed, for distortion grows from the child's guilt about his own sadistic phantasies. We can see examples of this as therapists, when a patient may begin therapy telling of a horrible childhood with an unloving mother and finishes therapy with a somewhat different view of a more human mother, a view less distorted by the unconscious phantasies of childhood. Or a patient who finds the concept of a break completely acceptable until within his internal world the good object becomes punitive through his own projections, leading to pathological manifestations of separation anxiety. In such an extreme case, a patient's internal world can become fragmented if the integration of being "held" by the Winnicottian concept of the good enough mother fails, leading to anxiety of loss of self and defensive somatisation, splitting, or acting out.

When trust is not yet sufficiently developed and patients have not internalised enough of the good object to enable separations and partings to be less devastating, the constant breaks in the therapeutic process provide us with an opportunity to discover the anxiety around separation, interpret it each time it is manifested and help the patient to mourn a loss and work through the anxiety. Because separation anxiety is a universal phenomenon that to varying degrees accompanies us all throughout life, it can become so familiar that it can almost be overlooked. Observing a very young child attempting to master it can be a useful reminder. Severe separation trauma in the first year of life can cause irreparable damage; in the second year, despite its comparable severity, psychotherapy may be able to help. We are constantly reminded in clinical practice, of patients' anxiety around loss and separation as it surfaces in the transference; this needs to be made conscious as they remember past separations. Gradually they struggle to reach a place where they are comfortable in the knowledge that they are separate from their therapist, unique as a person and secure in their own identity. For our patients, the final separation of finishing therapy is the ultimate loss after a process of experiencing repeated losses and it can only be really satisfactorily attained through constant interpretation. Ending therapy is dealt with in another chapter in this book. Here I am concentrating more on the difficulties, familiar to all psychotherapists, of patients' responses to breaks, from weekend breaks, to holiday breaks. Our "third ear" needs to be finely tuned to hear what patients are really saying when we give holiday break dates. It can be easy not to hear the latent content, or sometimes collude with the denials.

"It feels like school's out" said one patient, "it'll be quite a relief not to have my sessions." For me too, I thought. It had been a difficult few months' work with a new patient. The same patient anxiously telephoned at the end of the first week of the break, to check the exact date I was to be back. He had found, to his surprise, that he had a great deal he needed urgently to tell me. In terms of Bion's theory of container/contained, the container had gone. But it took time for him to acknowledge that the break reminded him of real separation at age five when his mother went back to work. His defence against anxiety was denial, but his telephone call gave the clue and enabled us to work on it. Another patient laughed derisively when I quietly wondered if his sudden severe headache might have something to do with the coming break. "You therapists are all the same." (He had been in therapy previously.) "You think everything revolves around you...". His anger became quite destructive and led to him missing the first two sessions after the break and then remaining silent on the couch. I felt this showed his internal conflict whereby his anger at not being able to control his therapist's disappearance led to him becoming cut off and silent, together with the depressed child who felt abandoned and possibly guilty. I was reminded of the small child who, in his despair at the mother's absence and anger at being unable to control her going, cannot bring to mind her image and becomes temporarily lost to affective human contact. This patient's somatising response to anxiety became quite acute during his therapy.

Freud describes such anxiety as being a response to the feelings of psychical and biological helplessness in the absence of the mother. Bowlby (1973, p. 26) describes a child's separation from mother as exhibiting three phases, protest, despair and detachment; the patient quoted above showed something of each of these phases.

One common response of patients on their return after a break is a euphoric first session; patient and therapist are pleased to meet again, to resume work, each replenished after some time away. After all, in families, even the most devoted mother needs time for herself and a developing child also needs his space. So the argument goes and the first session back can seem to confirm it. The next session apparently turns the argument on its head. Rage, confusion, reproaches or silence can greet the therapist, who in turn can be caught unawares and become confused. As sessions continue, perhaps understanding deepens. The patient's pleasure at seeing the therapist reflects his relief at realising that his rage at a perceived abandonment has not destroyed her; now it is safe to allow the anger to be voiced. Having given himself up to the pleasure of seeing the therapist again, secure in the knowledge that his omnipotent murderous rage has not had the desired/dreaded effect, he can get in touch with the feelings.

Anxiety about a separation *consciously* felt, produces sadness or anger, frustration, a feeling of being abandoned; if this can be expressed because a patient has learned to trust the therapist (as a child developmentally learns that its mother generally does return), the anxiety can gradually begin to be worked through. If, on the other hand, the anxiety seems too much to contain, unconscious mechanisms take over and defences such as repression, denial and splitting the ego are employed. This can lead to acting out behaviour, the patient unaware of the cause of his difficulties. As Brenman put it,

> He may indulge in loveless sexuality, stuff himself with food, drink, hatred, criticism and grievances to comfort himself. He may ... occupy himself with paranoid activity, physical fitness, hypochondriasis ... Separation is not consciously recognised. [1982, pp. 14–23]

A patient pre-empted my break by suddenly deciding to go away on a very glamorous holiday before I was going and coming back after I started work. We gradually understood how she felt more in control, how it "stopped the hurt" of the memory of being sent away to boarding school; this in turn overlaid a deep fear of being a refugee (as her parents had been), sent away from country and culture, a fear that was trans-generational in her family.

Other responses to separation anxiety, conscious and unconscious, are observed by all psychotherapists. A patient will check the dates many times and yet "forget" the first session back. Another patient forgets the break is 2 weeks long and comes back after 1 week. As a weekend break approaches, a patient in intensive therapy "remembers" a dream at the end of the Friday session, still recounting it as she puts on her coat and goes out of the door. Some acting out responses can be destructive. Because a patient feels abandoned by the therapist, he can allow a situation to develop within a relationship to spoil it, or become physically ill, or have an accident.

For one patient the breaks were so painful that the whole process of therapy was put in jeopardy as he angrily threatened to finish the work if I persisted in taking such holidays. His anger at my perceived cruelty became a destructive cycle. All interpretations, about the attack on himself, the therapy and the therapist, met with blankness. I noted how stuck and angry I felt in the countertransference, acknowledged the projections (to myself) and then understood how my interpretations had centred on his negativity and his anger, ignoring the attachment which made the separation so unbearable. During his angry silence, I said it must be very hard for him to acknowledge the attachment to me that made the breaks so painful. It was probably easier to be angry. It did not make him feel so vulnerable. He stayed silent, but the difference in the quality of the silence was palpable. Breaks continued to be an issue but he began to talk about his feelings of loss with sadness, not just anger; somehow the linking of the attachment with the angry paranoid feelings allowed him to move on. It had been a power struggle in which, until the element of sadness was interpreted, the patient was only able to respond to his feeling of helplessness.

As these sorts of responses to separation anxiety are familiar to all therapists in practice, perhaps they need to be put into a theoretical context. Freud's ideas on anxiety were developed throughout his writings. As early as 1905, in talking about infantile anxiety, he says, "Anxiety in children is originally nothing other than an expression of the fact that they are feeling the loss of the person they love," (1905c, p. 224). He based this on his observation of the child who was afraid of the dark, which Freud concluded was anxiety about the absence of the loved object. As soon as his mother made her presence known, he was calm. However, Freud's original theoretical explanation of anxiety was that of the unsatisfied libido manifested as anxiety and it was not until 1926 in "Inhibitions, Symptoms and Anxiety" (SE XX) that he finally stated that in his view it is the *fear* of separation and loss that is the cause of anxiety. Between these two theories and part of the development of his ideas on separation anxiety, came his writing in 1917 on the origins of depressive illness in "Mourning and Melancholia" (SE 14). He states that depression originates from a splitting of the ego, one part of which introjects the lost object, in conflict with the attacking other part, so the sadistic attack on the object is turned back on to the subject. But he adds what is so relevant for the therapist: "The patients still succeed, by the circuitous path of self-punishment, in taking revenge on the original object and in tormenting their loved one through their illness, having resorted to it in order to avoid the need to express their hostility to him openly." (1917, p. 251). This can be observed clearly in patients with a punitive superego who may, for instance, deprive themselves quite severely during a break, turning their anger with the therapist back on to themselves, thereby masking it and making it of critical importance to interpret.

Looking at separation anxiety from a Kleinian perspective, we know that Melanie Klein postulates that anxiety is the person's response to the death instinct. The infant perceives the object and ego separately right from birth, and anxiety is either persecutory (paranoid schizoid position) or depressive (depressive position). Thus anxiety may be experienced

> ... in a paranoid way, as the object turning back and attacking, or in a depressive way—that is, the object remains good and the anxiety concerns losing the good rather than being attacked by the bad. [Segal, 1979, p. 131]

According to Klein, the first anxiety felt by the infant is annihilation by the death instinct which is then projected outside and later is experienced as the persecutory bad object. The fear of annihilation has some similarities to Freud's 1926 postulation of unmastered anxiety threatening to overwhelm the infant's ego. In the paranoid–schizoid position, the unconscious phantasy is that self and idealised object may be destroyed, leading to schizoid defences of splitting, denial and idealisation being employed. In the depressive position, the infant fears his own sadistic destructiveness that might annihilate the loved object, on whom he is so dependent and who might disappear. After all, the mother does go away. Gradually, if the infant is psychically thriving, he introjects the whole good object, can remember his love for his mother even while hating her, can mourn her loss, secure in the feeling that she will return *and* that he has not destroyed her. In the paranoid–schizoid position, the guilt is so overwhelming, it attacks and destroys. In the depressive position it leads to reparation. With our patients, we can see how they can fluctuate between the two positions during therapy. A patient may feel independent and look forward to a break and also the resumption of the work with the therapist on returning and yet at another time, view an impending break with suspicion and anxiety. Klein emphasises the need always to be aware of and interpret separation anxiety *whenever* it appears, in the context of the whole transference situation, past history and present circumstances. As the transference is constantly fluctuating, so is it understood and reflected in the countertransference. This crucial line of communication must be kept open, to avoid stasis and a session degenerating into a meaningless hour of possible platitude.

> A patient found a new boyfriend just before or during a break and for some time I colluded with her, pleased, I thought, that this man might become a partner. Instead of being able to link the timing of her new, displaced attachment with the break and her dependence on and attachment to me, I allowed the sessions to become almost meaningless; the communication was truly blocked. The patient helped me see things more clearly and interpret appropriately by bringing a dream where I was thinly disguised as an intrusive yet complacent mother, allowing me to see how I was colluding with her displacement and acting out in order to appear to be the benevolent mother. When the latest relationship foundered she wept, mourning both the loss of the man and also the loss of her defence, which had protected her from acknowledging the separation from me. But because I was able this time to interpret in the here and now, not ignoring her defensive manoeuvres, proper communication was resumed and the lines were no longer crossed. My patient had been trying to cope with her feelings of helplessness, her sense of humiliation at being left and her indignation that I might be going to have an exciting (possibly sexual) time without her. Her terror of being alone was mixed with her envy of what she fantasised I might be doing. In defensively finding a man, she would not be alone and had no need to envy me.

Quinodoz in "The Taming of Solitude" also feels strongly that separation anxiety must be detected and analysed as soon as it appears, partly to restore verbal communication where it has been lost—it is important to make an interpretation so that the patient can begin to work through the anxiety. He feels that separation anxiety before breaks "tend(s) to disturb the process of working through by occasioning anxiety reactions and recourse to regressive defences, which have the effect of interrupting verbal communication between analysand and analyst for a greater or lesser period." (Quinodoz, 1993). Furthermore he feels that manifestations of loss and separation anxiety provide a unique opportunity to discover hidden aspects of the transference, "... the state of the analysand's object relations, his modes of defence, aspects of his personality which have remained split off, and his capacity to tolerate psychical pain, anxiety or mourning." (Quinodoz, 1993). Patients near the depressive position, in Kleinian terms, will be able to communicate their distress and accept a transference interpretation; it will make sense in terms of the work. A patient, smiling ruefully at "the human condition" she found herself in, feeling rather lost and abandoned, nevertheless felt able to let me go to my other life, knowing she was not forgotten. We both realised how much had been achieved when she was able to wish me a good holiday. On the other hand, for those patients for whom there is no perceived connection between what they are feeling and the therapist's break, the response will be primitive defence mechanisms manifested often in a completely flat affect. This can be a most difficult problem to grapple with. It can result in an interpretation as flat as the patient's affect, which of course has no resonance for the patient and is therefore useless at worst and banal at best.

A patient mentioned before, sometimes in touch with his anger around breaks, "retreated" into a distressing (for me) silence once after returning from a break. I had linked the silence with the break in a poor interpretation and his response was, "Yes, you would think that ...", in a completely flat voice. I could sense the despair but felt unable to reach it. One session that week he arrived late, which was unusual, explaining in a passive way that he had to take his small child to the nursery as his wife had left early for work. I said it felt as if he was unable to reach his feelings about this but that I thought it might feel something like the break when I "left him holding the baby" of his despair. He could not verbally acknowledge that this made any sense but something seemed to shift. A few sessions later we referred to the subject of his silences and he was able to articulate better (communication lines restored). He said that break dates make him feel at first helpless (the infant *is* helpless and dependent in the face of adult decisions) and then like jumping up from the couch and rushing from the room (mobilising acting out defences). Then he would be angrily silent or passively silent. The latter was compounded by my "predictable" interpretation which felt meaningless and which at least had the positive effect of making him angry again. Working with the ambivalent feelings, so that he became aware of the link between attachment and feared loss allowed him gradually to acknowledge separation in his life with less fear of catastrophe ensuing. In being silent, the patient assumed he had the power to punish me or make me anxious, which in reality had led to a meaningless interpretation. This justified his anger. "If you leave me holding the baby and don't hold me I'll be silent." But this in turn made him feel guilty until his attachment to his therapist was interpreted.

A problem that can occur is with patients whom we only see once weekly. Reaching separation anxiety can be much harder for the therapist. Manifestations are usually more obvious in intensive work with its regular structure and time frame. Constant separations may cause the intimacy of affect to be lost and make it much easier for the patient to simply disavow the existence of any feelings of anxiety. However, one needs to recognise that for all patients, on some level, any interruption in the therapeutic process indicates that the therapist has another life outside the consulting room, which forces the patient to look at his own relative importance in the therapist's life. This must apply to all patients, regardless of the intensity of sessions. But in less intensive therapy its importance can more easily be ignored or simply not noticed by therapist and patient alike and, in my opinion, one needs to be ever alert to its manifestation. Sometimes indications can be picked up at the beginning of the session with a patient anxiously "forgetting" what was discussed last week, revealing a lack of trust in the therapist being able to remember. Working intensively with other patients allows the therapist to become sensitive to separation anxiety and its manifestations and able to recognise the pointers. It is not only holiday breaks that can be so painful but also weekends, when the therapist "goes away", often to a fantasised sexual other life, leading to oedipal conflicts—the weekend, in Greenson's view, is the primal scene from which the patient is excluded (1967, p. 332)—or even between sessions, so the therapist needs to be sensitive to the altered rhythm of a session, paying special attention to the beginning and the end.

"Whichever object-relations theory is taken as one's basis, the working through of separation anxiety is a turning point and a pivotal stage in the psychoanalytic process" (Quinodoz, 1993, p. 33). If psychoanalytic psychotherapy is seen as a process within which a patient may develop into a more integrated person, who is independent and autonomous, it follows that containment of anxiety and an ability to tolerate separation and loss without resorting to primitive destructive defence mechanisms must be the aim and the challenge. Segal would put it in terms of the patient's capacity to move between the paranoid–schizoid and depressive positions, able to tolerate separation, with secure internal objects as points of reference. Another way of viewing it is that of André Green (1975, p. 17), who says, "Perhaps analysis only aims at the patient's capacity to be alone (in the presence of the analyst)", thereby linking Winnicott's formulation for the developing thriving infant with our hopes and aims for our patients. As psychoanalysis has changed its emphasis from Freud's original concept of making the unconscious conscious, towards the idea of working towards psychic change through the transference relationship, so the therapist sees that change can only be brought about through dealing with and helping the patient work through his separation anxiety. This includes mourning for the lost object throughout life from the trauma of birth separation and weaning, through the myriad of separations that accompany development. Within the microcosm of an analysis, we hope to enable the patient to re-experience the separations and acknowledge the anxiety which will be interpreted in the transference. The losses can then be mourned. The therapist must try to help the patient in the transition from a narcissistic way of relating to an object-relations way; from regressive responses, often denying the importance or indeed the existence of the therapist in the break, to responses acknowledging the attachment, negative and positive, to the therapist in terms of interpersonal relationships and thereby tolerating the ambivalence.

As we saw with the 2-year old child, internalising the presence of the good object replenishes his energies. Throughout therapy, this process can be seen happening in the context of the successive separations which evoke anxiety, with its attendant defences. If an interpretation is right, the patient is gradually able to internalise the object, enabling movement forward, with the realisation that the object is not destroyed by his phantasies. Anxiety does not disappear but may be contained and used in a positive affirmation of living, with the growing ability to tolerate and indeed enjoy separateness with a feeling of autonomy and an internal sense of security.

CHAPTER THIRTEEN

Termination and the resolution of the transference

Mary Twyman

"What we call the beginning is often the end
And to make an end is to make a beginning.
The end is where we start from."

"Four Quartets", Little Gidding, T. S. Eliot

On approaching the topic of termination in psychoanalysis and psychotherapy, it is immediately apparent that the area opened up for discussion is an important one for a number of reasons. Beginning to think about endings marks a particular point in treatment after which, in a real and essential way, things can never be the same again. Further, the fact of the imminence of ending in both the analyst's mind and that of the patient brings a particular atmosphere to the arena of the analytic work. What we know of the properties of the unconscious includes its capacity to maintain a sense of timelessness, even in the face of a reality that indicates otherwise and we can speculate that the unconscious resistance to the reality of an approaching ending cannot but increase when the ending of a lengthy analytic therapy is planned. The conscious, reflective, comparatively mature aspects of the ego of the patient who, in the most desirable situation, is anticipating ending as appropriate and has participated in the planning of the ending with the analyst, can be seriously at odds with unconscious elements that are responding to a very different agenda. While material might present that can be addressed throughout the termination time, there may remain elements that can never be fully addressed and may make themselves evident in the patient's life through enactments after the ending of the analysis. Of these the analyst is likely to know nothing. For it is one of the striking paradoxes of our work, that after perhaps years of intense analytic work with a patient, after the goodbyes of the final session, analyst and patient leave each other's lives for ever.

This is not to ignore the fact that patients return, perhaps just to see that the analyst survives, and to show that the patient has survived the trauma of ending, having faced the task of mourning alone. Sometimes patients return for a few sessions, perhaps at a time of crisis, for example at the time of the break-up of an important relationship, or when there has been a significant change of some kind in personal or professional life. The success and usefulness of these usually brief re-encounters can be variable. In my experience much depends on the degree to which the ending has been prepared for by both partners in the analytic dyad and for the patient especially, the fate of the analyst as a figure in the patient's mind. Here, largely, it is a matter of how far the inevitable ambivalence surrounding the final separation has been worked through in the course of the patient's psychic development since the ending. Where the good and the gain of the analysis has been not only maintained but allowed to continue its growth in the patient's mind, such brief contacts are usually fruitful; they represent a kind of coda to the symphony of the already completed analytic work. Where disappointment, incapacity for gratitude and the resentful preservation of grievance persist, it is unlikely that a brief postanalytic interlude will have much useful effect. It may serve only to confirm the patient's dissatisfaction with the analysis and the analyst.

Freud was ruefully aware of this sort of incidence. In "Analysis Terminable and Interminable" (1937b) he cites the patient who criticizes his former analyst to his present, second analyst, for incompletely analysing his negative transference. He also describes the fate of a woman patient who faced various set-backs and latterly physical illness after the end of her analysis with him; this precipitated a further bout of emotional illness which proved to be intractable to further analysis. I find Freud's comments on this case touchingly modest and a salutary example of his insistence on not making extravagant claims for psychoanalysis, even, perhaps especially, at this late stage in his life.

> The successful analytic treatment took place so long ago that we cannot expect too much from it; it was in the earliest years of my work as an analyst. No doubt the patient's second illness may have sprung from the same source as her first one which had been successfully overcome; it may have been a different manifestation of the same repressed impulses, which the analysis had only incompletely resolved. But I am inclined to think that, were it not for the new trauma, there would have been no fresh outbreak of neurosis [p. 222]

Plainly and honestly he comments: ... "she remained abnormal to the end of her life" (p. 222).

It strikes me that what Freud puts into words here is likely to resonate with analysts as they reflect on the endings of analyses they have conducted. Have I done enough to enable the patient to live creatively from now on? How do I know? What are my limitations, what are the patient's? What has changed for the patient, what has not? Does the patient know of and accept that in himself which has not been altered by the analysis, can he bear a degree of disillusionment? Can I accept my limitations and how, by being the analyst I am, I may have failed this patient in certain ways? While the duration of analyses in contemporary practice usually exceeds those carried out by Freud and his associates, we might expect that we have a greater opportunity and indeed obligation to be thorough. But we face the same dilemmas as Freud and his contemporaries. Later in the same paper Freud reflects "... optimists ... assume that there really is a possibility of disposing of an instinctual conflict (or more correctly, a conflict between the ego and an instinct) definitively and for all time" (p. 223). He makes it clear that he is not among the optimists and that the questions raised about the long-term effectiveness of analysis to "... inoculate him [the patient] against the possibility of any such conflicts ..." (p. 223) are ones that he does not propose to answer and which he doubts can have certain answers at all, but that the direction in which they may be found lies in the area of theoretical considerations, not least of which is the length of treatment. Do the longer treatments that are now the norm in psychoanalysis and psychoanalytic psychotherapy yield any answers to Freud's questions?

Perhaps the indications lie in the attention that is now afforded to the process of termination. Although we cannot speak of a typical analysis, there are certain phases in analytic work that are recognizable to most practitioners. The early phase, the beginning, taking up perhaps the first year or 18 months when patient and analyst are getting to know one another. Nina Coltart (1992) writes about this time as one in which the analyst is "... feeling for the available transferences," (p. 7) an acute and telling phrase. She writes that she often wished to get over the first year of an analysis, knowing that the substantive work of the analysis could not really begin until the preliminary work of establishing the patient's trust in the analyst and the analytic process had occurred. There is a time in the beginning phase when it is possible to recognize that the patient's unconscious mind has become engaged in the analytic work and the momentum of the analytic encounter quickens; the work can then deepen. It is then that the central work of the analysis is launched. It could be thought of as being like the middle game in chess, or the development section in a movement of a sonata-form symphonic composition, in which all the themes that appear in the exposition (or in our work, in the early phase of the analysis) are woven and elaborated in a complex pattern of repetition and reiteration. Yet always something new emerges, a revelation but with certain familiar features of the original themes. What is alive in the transference is the surest guide to understanding the nature and status of these themes, which are central to the patient. It is in the myriad shifts in the transference that the analyst can gauge when the intimations for termination begin to appear.

It may be that the patient begins to think and speak of a time in the future when he can imagine ending the analysis. He may well, having mentioned this, let it drop for a while, but the analyst will have noted it. It marks a shift, a recognition of the finiteness of the analytic encounter, the potentiality for acknowledging the inevitability of a final separation. The patient registers psychic change in himself, change that is often unexpected, different from the idealized, omnipotent expectations he may have held for himself and for the analytic process. The acceptance of the actual change as an achievement and a gain can be a source of satisfaction.

One patient in the ending phase of an analysis spoke of a surprising sense of freedom that stemmed from something she had identified as a sense of *acceptance* which she had hitherto associated only with reluctance, as referring to a thing imposed which she would resist. Her emotional freedom gained after years of analytic work coincided with an acceptance of herself, more fully engaged and effective in her relationships, more creative and imaginative in her working and living than had ever seemed possible previously. It goes without saying that this acceptance derived from the sustained accepting of all manifestations of herself in the analytic encounter.

Another woman patient in the final phase of a 6-year analysis had moved from being severely depressed and living a much restricted life, to finding increasing satisfaction in acquiring new skills, studying, writing, painting and travelling as well as freeing herself from a limpet-like identification with her depressed mother. Access to her aggression and feelings of hatred had been at the heart of the "middle game" stage of her analysis, and in the final phase this was turned towards her analyst who had hitherto been shielded from these aspects of herself in a somewhat stifling idealizing transference. This took the form of angry attacks on the analyst for not having done enough, for not transforming her into the super-achieving woman she wanted to be. Throughout this time she was struggling with finding an ordinary, good enough, object in her analyst which she could internalize and which could help her to appreciate what had been achieved in the course of the treatment. She feared returning to her depressed state after the ending and accused her analyst of failing to banish forever her occasional depressed moods. Yet in her final sessions she was able both to stand her ground on her complaints and also to acknowledge that she was being unfair, that she was sad to be leaving, that she was appreciative and grateful for the help she had received, and that she had confidence that she would remain well. A brief meeting a year later confirmed that she had indeed sustained the improved state.

In my experience the ending phase of an analysis may include sections which are rather quiet and reflective, with patient and analyst reviewing the relationship and what has happened in the time they have spent together. There are the patient's phantasies of the extra-analytic relationship, both conscious and also often making an appearance in dreams.

A woman patient brought a dream of walking hand-in-hand with her (male) analyst in a quiet district of the city which she associated with her analyst's early life, i.e. life before she had been his patient. She revealed her affection for her analyst, her almost-renounced erotic wishes in relation to him and a longing to have been part of his life before, and by implication, after the analysis.

A male patient, coming towards ending, reminded his (female) analyst of a dream he had had after his first meeting with the analyst. He dreamt he was lying on the couch in her consulting room and beside her on a shelf was a baby. In retrospect he saw this dream as predictive of what needed to happen in the analysis; he needed something in the analytic encounter that allowed the infantile self to come down off the shelf.

These calm, on-track phenomena have to be contrasted with the more turbulent events which can mark the termination phase. Return of symptoms which have in the past yielded to analytic understanding can be a problematic feature, alarming to both patient and analyst. Depressive, regressive episodic reactions with a recurrence of physical symptoms that may have dominated earlier phases in the analysis, can bring pressure upon the analyst to extend the work beyond the fixed ending date. Firmness is needed in these circumstances for it is only by sticking to what has been agreed that the still necessary work of pursuing the meaning of such symptoms, in the light now of ending, can be done. It remains, however, a striking paradox that the analytic relationship, with its exclusivity, intimacy and sheer intensity comes to an end in a more-or-less abrupt fashion. There is no way round this. Nina Coltart (1993) writes in her book *How to Survive as a Psychotherapist*:

> It is perfectly possible to bring about changes in the ego by means of dynamic therapy such that it is forever stronger, more resilient, more able to cope with, among other things, severe separation pain. But beyond a certain point, it is not possible to anticipate (in order to protect against) the actual experience of loss [p. 10].

We can and do as analysts work towards this phenomenon we call resolution of the transference, but the essence of this experience is the patient's alone, achieved, if it is, without us. While the patient is engaged in the complex tasks of gradually de-cathecting the object he is about to leave and making preparation for a different kind of identification with his analyst and with the analytic process, what happens to the analyst?

John Klauber (1981) in *Difficulties in the Analytic Encounter* has written with great sensitivity of the analyst's experience, on-going as the treatment proceeds and in the course of ending. He writes:

> ... the analyst needs the patient in order to crystallize and communicate his own thoughts, including some of his inmost thoughts on intimate human problems which can only grow organically in the context of this relationship [p. 51].

Here he touches on the issue of the analyst's loss of communication with a particular patient as the analysis comes to an end. He mentions also other aspects that can affect both analyst and patient. He notes that it is not uncommon for patients to harbour resentment towards former analysts and remarks that among other causes for this may be what he refers to as the "tease" inherent in the stimulation and frustration of emotions in the analytic relationship. He notes also that there may be a temptation for analysts to sabotage their relationship with patients after termination. He points out the difficulty in countertransference feeling that this might denote, adding, "After all how can we be expected to allow patients to impose so much instinctual restraint on us and not to resent them for it?" (p. 57).

These observations usher in an enquiry into the long-term effect of analytic work on the analyst and especially in respect of the analyst's mourning for his patients. He is quick to point out that this process is not comparable with the patient's mourning process following termination, yet the ending of an analysis and the concerned involvement it has entailed for the analyst may well give rise to some form of introjection to make up for the loss of the satisfying experience that has ended. In Zygmunt Bauman's (1993) powerful phrase which to me sums up the peculiar nature of the analytic relationship, the analyst experiences "the unbearable silence of responsibility".

REFERENCES

Abraham, K. (1917). The spending of money in anxiety states. In: *Selected Papers of Karl Abraham, 1949*. London: Hogarth Press. Contributions to the theory of the anal character. *International Journal of Psycho-analysis, 1923, 1*: 400–418.

Abram, J. (1996). *The Language of Winnicott*. London: Karnac Books.

Alanen, Y. O. (1997). *Schizophrenia. Its Origins and Need-Adapted Treatment, Chap. 3*. London: Karnac Books.

Alvarez, A. (1992). *Live Company*. London and New York: Tavistock/Routledge.

Alvarez, A. (1999). Frustration and separateness, delight and connectedness: reflections on the condition under which good and bad surprises are conducive to learning. *Journal of Child Psychotherapy, 25*: 183–198.

Archer, S. (1993). Shame, guilt and counterfeiting. *Journal of the British Association of Psychotherapists, 24*. Revised: *Australian Journal of Psychotherapy, 15* (1): 1996.

Auerhahn, N. C. (1979). Interpretation in the psychoanalytic narrative: a literary framework for the psychoanalytic process. *International Review of Psycho-Analysis, 6*: 423–436.

Baker, R. (1993). Some reflections on humour in psychoanalysis. *International Journal of Psychoanalysis, 74:* 951–960.

Baker, R. (1993). The patient's discovery of the psychoanalyst as a new object. *International Journal of Psycho-Analysis, 74:* 1223–1233.

Balint, M. (1969). Trauma and object relationship. *International Journal of Psycho-Analysis, 50:* 429–4.

Bauman, Z. (1993). *Postmodern Ethics.* Oxford: Blackwell.

Bergler, E. (1956). *Homosexuality: Disease or Way of Life.* New York: Collier Books.

Berkowitz, R. (1999). The potential for trauma in the transference and countertransference. In: S. Johnson & S. Ruszczynski (Eds.), *Psychoanalytic Psychotherapy in the Independent Tradition.* London: Karnac Books.

Berman I. et al. (1998). Obsessions and compulsions as a distinct cluster of symptoms in schizophrenia: a neuropsychological study. *Journal of Nervous Mental Disorders, 186:* 150–156.

Bion, W. R. (1959). Attacks on Linking. *Second Thoughts.* London: Maresfield. Reprints. (1967a) *International Journal of Psycho-Analysis, 40* (5–6): 1959.

Bion, W. (1962). *Learning from Experience.* Heinemann.

Bion, W. R. (1992). *Cogitations.* London: Karnac Books.

Bion, W. R. (1967). Selected Papers on Psychoanalysis. *Second Thoughts.* Maresfield Reprints: London.

Bion, W. R. (1978). *Four Discussions.* Perthshire: Clunie P.

Bion, W. R. (1980). *Bion in New York and Sao Paulo.* Perthshire: Clunie Press.

Bollas, C. (2000). *Hysteria.* London and New York: Routledge.

Booth, W. C. (1991). *The Rhetoric of Fiction.* Penguin Books.

Bowlby, J. (1973). *Attachment and Loss, Vol. 2.* London: Hogarth Press and the Institute of Psycho-Analysis.

Brafman, A. H. (1997). Winnicott's "Therapeutic Consultations Revisited". *International Journal of Psycho-Analysis, 78:* 773–787.

Brafman, A. H. (2001). *Untying the Knot—Working with Children and Parents.* London and New York: Karnac.

Braunwald, E., Fauci, A. S., Kasper, D. L., Hauser, S. L., Longo, D. L., & Jameson, J. L. (2001). *Harrison's Principles of Internal Medicine, 15th Edition.* New York: McGraw Hill.

Brenman, E. (1982). Separation: a clinical problem. *Bulletin of the British Psycho-Analytical Society, 1:* 14–23.

Brenman Pick, I. (1985). Working through in the counter-transference. In: E. B. Spillius (Ed.), *Melanie Klein Today, Vol. 2: Mainly Practice*. London: Routledge.

Breuer, J., & Freud, S. (1893–95) (1955). Studies in Hysteria. In: *The Standard Edition of the Complete Psychological Works of Sigmund Freud, Vol. 2*. London: Hogarth Press.

Britton, R. S. (1989). The missing link: parental sexuality in the Oedipus Complex. In: *The Oedipus Complex To-day—Clinical Implications*. London: Karnac Books.

Bryer, I. (1962). *The Heart to Artemis*. New York: Harcourt, Brace & World.

Campbell, D (1999). The role of the father in a pre-suicide state. In: R. J. Perelberg (Ed.), *Psychoanalytic Understanding of Violence and Suicide* (pp. 73–86). London and New York: Routledge.

Carpy, Denis V. (1989). Tolerating the countertransference: a mutative process. *International Journal of Psychoanalysis, 70*: 287–294.

Carroll, L. (1906). *Alice's Adventures in Wonderland*. London: MacMillan and Co. Ltd.

Casement, P. (1985). *On Learning from the Patient*. London and New York: Tavistock Publications.

Chasseguet-Smirgel, J. (1985a). *The Ego Ideal*. London: Free Association.

Chasseguet-Smirgel, J. (1985b). *Creativity and Perversion*. London: Free Association.

Coltart, N. (1987). Diagnosis and assessment of suitability for psychoanalytical psychotherapy. *British Journal of Psychotherapy, 4* (2): 127–134.

Coltart, N. (1992). *Slouching Towards Bethlehem*. London: Free Association Books.

Coltart, N. (1993). *How to Survive as a Psychotherapist*. London: Sheldon Press.

Cooper, J. (1993). *Speak of Me as I am: The Life and Work of Masud Khan*. London: Karnac Books.

Couch, A. S. (1992). Personal communication. In: J. Cooper (Ed.), *Speak of Me as I am: The Life and Work of Masud Khan*. London: Karnac Books.

Couch, A. S. (1995). Anna Freud's adult psychoanalytic technique: a defence of classical analysis. *International Journal of Psycho-Analysis, 76*: 153–171.

Couch, A. S. (1999). Therapeutic functions of the real relationship in psychoanalysis. *The Psychoanalytic Study of the Child, 54*: 130–168.

Crow, T. J. (1991). The origins of psychosis and the "descent of man". *British Journal of Psychiatry, 159* (suppl. 14): 76–82.

Crow, T. J. (1997). Temporolimbic or transcallosal connection: where is the primary lesion in schizophrenia and what is its nature. *Schizophrenia Bulletin, 23* (3): 521–523.

Cullberg J. et al. (2000). Integrating intensive psychosocial and low-dose neuroleptic treatment: a three-year follow-up. In: B. Martindale, A. Bateman, M. Crowe & F. Margison (Eds.), *Psychosis. Psychological Approaches and Their Effectiveness.* Gaskell, Glasgow: Bell & Bain Ltd.

D. S. M. VI. (2000). *Diagnostic and Statistical Manual of Mental Disorders, 4th Edition.* Washington D.C.: American Psychiatric Association.

Drescher, J. (1995). Anti-homosexual bias in training. In: *Disorientating Sexuality* (pp. 227–241). London and New York: Routledge.

Edelman, G. (1992). *Bright Air, Brilliant Fire—On the Matter of the Mind.* London: Penguin.

Edelman, G. (1994) (January 24th). *The Man Who Made Up His Mind.* Horizon, BBC TV Program and accompanying booklet. London: British Broadcasting Support Services.

Eissler, K. R. (1974). On some theoretical and technical problems regarding the payment of fees for psycho-analytic treatment. *International Review of Psycho-Analysis, 1*: 73–101.

Ellenberger, H. F. (1970). *The Discovery of the Unconscious.* New York: Basic Books.

Engel, G. E. (1975). The death of a twin: mourning and anniversary reactions. Fragments of 10 years of self-analysis. *International Journal of Psycho-Analysis, 56*: 38.

Erikson, E. H. (1950). *Childhood and Society.* London: Norton, New York, and Penguin.

Etchegoyen, R. H. (1991) (revised ed. 1999). *The Fundamentals of Psychoanalytic Technique.* London: Karnac Books.

Fairbairn, W. (1958). On the nature and aims of psychoanalytic treatment. *International Journal of Psycho-Analysis, 39*: 374–385.

Fairbairn, W. R. D. (1981). *Psychoanalytic Studies of the Personality. Chapters IV and VII.* London: Routledge & Kegan Paul.

Falloon, I. R. H. et al. (1996). Early detection and intervention for initial episodes of schizophrenia. *Schizophrenia Bulletin, 22,* (2).

Fenton, W. S. et al. (1986). The prognostic significance of obsessive–compulsive symptoms in schizophrenia. *American Journal of Psychiatry, 143* (4): 437–441.

Ferenczi, S. (1914). The ontogenesis of the interest in money. In: M. Balint (Ed.), E. Mosbacher (Trans.), *First Contributions to the Problems and Methods of Psycho-Analysis* (pp. 336–341). London: Hogarth Press, 1955. [Reprinted London: Karnac Books, 1994.]

Fox, R. P. (1984). The principle of abstinence reconsidered. *International Review of Psycho-Analysis, 11*: 227–236.

Freud, A. (1921). 'Letter to Eitingon on her discussions with Lou Salome'. Anna Freud; Elizabeth Young-Bruehl. London: Macmillan.

Freud, A. (1937). *The Ego and the Mechanisms of Defence*. London: Hogarth Press.

Freud, S. (1886–1889). Part 2 Psychopathology: the hysterical proton pseudos. In: J. Strachey (Ed.), *The Standard Edition of the Complete Psychological Works of Sigmund Freud, Vol. 2*. London: Hogarth Press.

Freud, S. (1897). Letter 29. *S.E. 1*: 272–273.

Freud, S. (1901–5). Fragment of an analysis of a case of hysteria ('Dora'). *S.E. 7*, p. 110.

Freud, S. (1903). 'Die Zeist' (Viennese Newspaper, October 27th) *The Psychoanalytic Theory of Male Homosexuality*. Kenneth Lewes. London and New York: Quartet Books.

Freud, S. (1905a). On Psychotherapy. *S.E. 7*, p. 233.

Freud, S. (1905b). Jokes and their relation to the unconscious. *S.E. 8*.

Freud, S. (1905c). Three essays on the theory of sexuality. *S.E. 7*.

Freud, S. (1908). Character and anal erotism. *S.E. 9*: 168–175.

Freud, S. (1912). Recommendations to physicians practicing psycho-analysis. *S.E. 12*.

Freud, S. (1913). On beginning the treatment. *S.E. 12*: 123–141.

Freud, S. (1914). On narcissism. *S.E. 14*.

Freud, S. (1915). Observations on transference-love. *S.E. 12*.

Freud, S. (1917 [1915]). Mourning and melancholia. *S.E. 14*.

Freud, S. (1919). Lines of advance in psychoanalytic theory. *S.E. 17*: 159–168.

Freud, S. (1923a). The ego and the id. *S.E. 19*.

Freud, S. (1923b). Neurosis and psychosis. *On Psychopathology, Vol. 10*. Penguin Books.

Freud, S. (1926). Inhibitions, symptoms and anxiety. *S.E. 20*.

Freud, S. (1927). Humour.

Freud, S. (1933 [1932]). The dissection of the psychical personality. *S.E. 22.*

Freud, S. (1935). Letters to an American mother. *American Journal of Psychiatry, 107:* 786.

Freud, S. (1937a). Constructions in analysis. *S.E. 23.*

Freud, S. (1937b). Analysis terminable and interminable. *S.E. 23.*

Freud, S. (1938). An outline of psychoanalysis. *S.E. 23.*

Freud, S., & Breuer, J. (1893). Studies on hysteria. *S.E. 2.*

Gabbard, G. O. (1997). Dynamic therapy in the decade of the brain. *Connecticut Medicine, 61* (9).

Gates, B. (1984). Behold this dreamer. In: W. de la Mare (Ed.), *Abnormal Psychology.* London: Faber and Faber.

Gill, M. M. (1967). The Primary Process. *Psychological Issues, 5* (2–3), monograph 18/19.

Gitelson, M. (1952). The emotional position of the analyst in the psycho-analytic situation. *International Journal of Psycho-Analysis, 33:* 1–10.

Glasser, M. (1985). Aspects of violence. Paper given to the Applied Section of the British Psycho-analytical Society.

Glover, E. (1955). *The Technique of Psychoanalysis.* New York: International Universities Press.

Goldman, D. (1993). *In Search of the Real.* Northvale, New Jersey and London: Jason Aronson.

Green, A. (1975). The analyst, symbolization and absence in the analytic setting. *International Journal of Psycho-Analysis, 56:* 1–22.

Greenberg, J. R., & Mitchell, S. A. (1983). *Object Relations in Psychoanalytic Theory, Part 2, Chap. 6.* Cambridge, Massachusetts, and London: Harvard University Press.

Greenough, W. T. et al. (1987). Experience and Brain Development. *Child Development, 58:* 539–559.

Greenson, R. R. (1960). Empathy and its vicissitudes 1. *International Journal of Psycho-Analysis, 41:* 418–424.

Greenson, R. R. (1967). *The Technique and Practice of Psycho-Analysis.* London: Hogarth.

Greenson, R. R. (1969). The origin and fate of new ideas in psycho-analysis. *International Journal of Psycho-Analysis, 50:* 503–515.

Greenson, R. R. (1978). *Explorations in Psychoanalysis.* New York: International Universities Press, Inc.

Grinberg, L. (1962). On a specific aspect of countertransference due to the patient's projective Identification. In: R. Langs (Ed.), *Classics in Psycho-Analytic Technique*. New York (1981): Aronson and also *International Journal of Psycho-Analysis, 43*: 436–440.

Groddeck, G. (1977). *The Meaning of Illness*. London: Hogarth Press.

Grotstein, J. S. (1994). Endopsychic structures and the cartography of the internal world: six endopsychic characters in search of an author. In: J. S. Grotstein & D. B. Rinsley (Eds.), *Fairbairn and the Origins of Object Relations*. New York and London: The Guildford Press.

Hamilton, M. (1976). Fish's Clinical Psychopathology (pp. 24, 29, 30–1). Bristol: John Wright and Sons Ltd.

Hamilton, V. (1996). *The Analyst's Preconscious*. Hilldale NJ/London: Analytic Press.

Haynal, A. (1993). Ferenczi and the origins of psychoanalytic technique. In: L. Aron & A. Harris (Eds.), *The Legacy of Sandor Ferenczi*. Hillsdale NJ and London: The Analytic Press.

Haynes, S., & Wiener, J. (1996). The analyst in the counting house: money as symbol and reality in analysis. *British Journal of Psychotherapy, 13* (1): 14–25.

Heiman, P. (1950). On counter-transference. *International Journal of Psycho-Analysis, 31*: 81–84. Reprinted in: *About Children and Children no Longer* (1989) pp. 73–79, In: M. Tonnesmann (Ed.). London: Routledge.

Heimann, P. (1978). On the necessity for the analyst to be natural with his patient. In: M. Tonnesmann (Ed.), *About Children and Children-No-Longer: Collected Papers 1942–80, Paula Heimann*. London: Routledge.

Herman, N. (1985). *My Kleinian Home*. London: Quartet Books.

Hinshelwood, R. D. (1999). Countertransference. *International Journal of Psychoanalysis, 80*: 797–818.

Hoffer, A. (1993). Ferenczi's relevance to contemporary psycho-analytic technique: commentary on Andre Haynal; Ferenczi and the origins of psychoanalytic technique. In: L. Aron & A. Harris (Eds.), *The Legacy of Sandor Ferenczi*. Hillsdale NJ and London: The Analytic Press.

Holmes, J. (1998). Money and psychotherapy: object, metaphor or dream. *International Journal of Psychotherapy, 3* (2): 123–133.

Hope, R. A., Longmore, J. M., McManus, S. K., & Wood-Allum, C.

A. (1998). *Oxford Handbook of Clinical Medicine, 4th Edition.* Oxford: Oxford University Press.

Horrobin, D. F. (1999). A speculative overview: the relationship between phospholipid spectrum disorders and human evolution. In: M. Peet et al. (Eds.), *Phospholipid Spectrum Disorder in Psychiatry.* Lancashire, U.K.: Marius Press.

Hurry, A. (Ed.). (1998). *Psychoanalysis and Developmental Therapy.* London: Karnac Books.

Hyatt-Williams, A. (1998). *Cruelty, Violence, and Murder. Understanding the Criminal Mind.* New Jersey, London: Jason Aronson Inc.

Jones, E. (1950). Anal-erotic character traits. In: *Papers on Psychoanalysis* (pp. 413–437). London: Bailliere, Tindale and Cox.

Joseph, B. (1975). Transference: the total situation. In: E. Bott Spillius (Ed.), *Melanie Klein Today, Vol. 2* (pp. 61–72). London: Tavistock/Routledge, 1988.

Kandel, E. R. (1999). Biology and the future of psychoanalysis: a new intellectual framework for psychiatry revisited. *American Journal of Psychiatry, 156* (4).

Kaplan-Solms, K., & Solms, M. (2000). *Clinical Studies in Neuro-Psychoanalysis.* London and New York: Karnac Books.

Kernberg, O. F. (1980). *Borderline Conditions and Pathological Narcissism, Part 1.* New York: Jason Aronson, Inc.

Kernberg, O. F. (1999). Psychoanalysis, psychoanalytical psychotherapy and supportive psychotherapy: contemporary controversies. *International Journal of Psychoanalysis, 80*: 1075–1092.

Khan, M. (1972). The use and abuse of dream in psychic experience. In: *The Privacy of the Self* (pp. 306–315). London: Hogarth Press, 1974.

King, P. (1978). Affective response of the analyst to the patient's communications. *International Journal of Psycho-Analysis, 59*: 329–334.

King, P., & Steiner, R. (1991). *The Freud–Klein Controversies 1941–1945.* London & New York: Tavistock/Routledge.

Kinston, W. (1980). A theoretical and technical approach to narcissistic disturbance. *International Journal of Psychoanalysis, 61*: 383–394.

Kinston, W. (1982). An intrapsychic developmental schema for narcissistic disturbance. *International Review of Psychoanalysis, 9*: 253–261.

Kinston, W. (1983). A theoretical context for shame. *International Journal of Psychoanalysis, 64*: 213–226.

Klauber, J. (1981). *Difficulties in the Analytic Encounter*. New York: Jason Aronson. [Reprinted London: Karnac Books, 1986.]

Klauber, J. (1987). *Illusion and Spontaneity in Psychoanalysis*. London: Free Association Books.

Klein, M. (1946). Notes on some schizoid mechanisms. In: *Envy and Gratitude and Other Works*. London: Hogarth Press and the Institute of Psychoanalysis (1984).

Klein, M. (1952). Some theoretical conclusions regarding the emotional life of the infant. *Envy and Gratitude and Other Works*. London: Hogarth Press and the Institute of Psychoanalysis (1984).

Klein, M. (1955). On identification. In: M. Klein, P. Heimann & R. Money-Kyrle (Eds.), *New Directions in Psycho-analyses*. London: Maresfield Reprints (1977).

Klein, M. (1957). Envy and gratitude. In: *Envy and Gratitude and Other Works 1946–63*. London: Hogarth Press, 1975.

Klein, M. (1975). Notes on some schizoid mechanisms (1946). *Envy and Gratitude, Chap. 1*. London: Hogarth Press and the Institute of Psychoanalysis (1984).

Kohon, G. (1999). Hysteria. In: *No Lost Certainties to Be Recovered, Chap. 1*. London: Karnac Books.

Laing, A. (1994). *R D Laing A Life*. London: Harper Collins (1994).

Laufer, E. (1987). Suicide in adolescence. *Psychoanalytic Psychotherapy, 3* (1): 1–10.

Leary, K. R. (1989) Psychoanalytic process and narrative process: a critical consideration of Shafer's 'narrational project'. *International Review of Psycho-Analysis, 16*: 179–190.

LeFevre, D. C., & Morrison, F. (1997). The Hawthorn Project. A group psychotherapy project with chronically psychotic inpatients. In: C. Mace & Margison (Eds.), *Psychotherapy of Psychosis*. Gaskell.

LeFevre, D. C. (1999). Psychotherapy training for nurses as part for a group psychotherapy project: the pivotal role of counter-transference. In: V. L. Schermer & M. Pines (Eds.), *Group Psychotherapy of the Psychoses, Chap. 13*. London and Philadelphia: Jessica Kingsley Publishers.

Lipton, S. (1977). The advantages of Freud's technique as shown in his analysis of the Rat Man. *International Journal of Psycho-Analysis, 58:* 255–273.

Lishman, W. A. (1980). *Organic Psychiatry. The Psychological Consequences of Cerebral Disorder* (p. 706). Oxford: Blackwell Scientific Publications.

Little, M. (1951). Counter-transference and the patient's response to it. *International Journal of Psycho-Analysis, 33:* 1–10.

Loewald, H. (1980). *Reflections on the psychoanalytic process and its therapeutic potential in "Papers on Psychoanalysis".* Newhaven and London: Yale University Press.

Lucas, R. (1998). Why the cycle in a cyclical psychosis? An analytic contribution to the understanding of recurrent manic–depressive psychosis. *Psychoanalytic Psychotherapy, 12* (3): 193–212.

Mahler et al. (1975). *The Psychological Birth of the Human Infant.* New York: Basic Books. [Reprinted London: Maresfield Library, 1985.]

Malin, A., & Grotstein, J. (1966) Projective identification in the therapeutic process. *International Journal of Psycho-Analysis 47:* 26–31; and also: R. Langs (Ed.), *Classics in Psycho-analytic Technique.* New York: Aronson (1981).

Maltzberger, J. G., & Buie, D. H. (1980). The devices of suicide. *International Review of Psycho-Analysis, 7:* 61–72.

Maugham, W. S. (1915). *Of Human Bondage.* New York: Maine Library.

McGorry, P. (2000). Psychotherapy and recovery in early psychosis: a core clinical and research challenge. In: B. Martindale, A. Bateman, M. Crowe & F. Margison (Eds.), *Psychosis: Psychological Approaches and their Effectiveness, Chap. 13.* Gaskell: Gaskell Bell and Bain Ltd.

Mellor, J. E. et al. (1996). Omega-3 fatty acid supplementation in schizophrenic patients. *Human Psychopharmacology, 11:* 39–46.

Meltzer, M. D. (1967). *The Psycho-Analytical Process.* Perthshire: Clunie Press. [Reprinted 1979.]

Menninger, K. (1958). *Theory of Psychoanalytic Technique.* New York: Basic Books.

Miller, S. B. (1985). *The Shame Experience.* New Jersey: The Analytic Press.

Miller, S. B. (1989). Shame as an impetus to the creation of conscience. *International Journal of Psychoanalysis, 70:* 231–242.

Mollon, P. (1984). Shame in relation to narcissistic disturbance. *British Journal of Medical Psychology, 57*: 207–214.

Mollon, P. (1999). *Multiple Selves, Multiple Voices, Chap. 1.* Chichester, New York, Brisbane, Toronto and Singapore: John Wiley and Sons.

Morris, H. Narrative representation, narrative enactment and the psychoanalytic construction of history. *International Journal of Psycho-Analysis, 74*: 33–54.

Nathanson, D. L. (1987). *The Many Faces of Shame.* New York and London: Guilford.

O'Shaughnessy, E. (1999). Relating to the superego. *The International Journal of Psychoanalysis, 80* (5): 861–870.

Ogden, T. H. (1994). *Subjects of Analysis.* London: Karnac Books.

Ogden, T. H. (1979). On projective identification. *International Journal of Psycho-Analysis, 60*: 357–373.

Olsson, P. A. (1986). Complexities in the psychology and psychotherapy of the phenomenally wealthy. In: D. W. Krueger (Ed.), *The Last Taboo.* New York: Bruner Kazel.

Peet, M. et al. (1999). *Phospholipid Spectrum Disorder in Psychiatry.* Lancashire, U.K.: Marius Press.

Perelberg, R. J. (1999). Psychoanalytic understanding of violence and suicide. *The New Library of Psychoanalysis, 33.* London and New York: Routledge.

Pick, I. (1985). Working through in the countertransference. *International Journal of Psycho-Analysis, 66*: 157–166.

Pines, M. (1987). Shame—what psychoanalysis does and does not say. *Journal of Group Analysis, 20*: 16–31.

Poland, W. (1998). Witnessing and others. *Journal of the American Psycho-analytic Association, 48* (1): 17–93.

Poyurovsky, M. D. et al. (1999). Obsessive–compulsive disorder in patients with first-episode schizophrenia. *American Journal of Psychiatry, 156*: 12.

Puri, B. K. et al. (2000). Eicosapentanenoic acid treatment in schizophrenia associated with symptom remission, normalisation of blood fatty acids, reduced neuronal membrane phospholipid turnover and structural brain change. *International Journal of Clinical Practice, 54* (1).

Quinodoz, J. M. Clinical facts or psychoanalytical clinical facts? *International Journal of Psycho-Analysis, 75*: 963–976.

Quinodoz, J.-M. (1993). *The Taming of Solitude*. London: Routledge.

Richards, J. (1993). Cohabitation and the negative therapeutic reaction. *Psychoanalytic Psychotherapy, 7* (3): 223–239.

Riviere, J. (1940). A character trait of Freud's. In: J. D. Sutherland (Ed.), *Psychoanalysis and Contemporary Thought*. London: Hogarth, 1958. [Reprinted London: Maresfield Library, Karnac Books, 1987.]

Robbins, M. (1993). *Experiences of Schizophrenia*. New York and London: The Guildford Press.

Rosenfeld, H. A. (1984). *Psychotic States, Chaps. 3 and 12*. London: Maresfield Reprints.

Ruitenbeek, H. M. (1973). Include the patient in your world. In: H. M. Ruitenbeek (Ed.), *The Analytic Situation*. Chicago: Aldine Publishing Company.

Rycroft, C. (1972). *A Critical Dictionary of Psychoanalysis*. London: Penguin.

Sandler, J. (1976). Countertransference and role responsiveness. *International Review of Psycho-Analysis, 3*: 43–47.

Schafer, R. (1976). *A New Language for Psychoanalysis*. New Haven: Yale University Press.

Schafer, R. (1983). *The Analytic Attitude*. London: Hogarth Press. [Reprinted London: Karnac Books, 1993.]

Searles, H. (1959). 'Oedipal love in the countertransference' *Collected papers on schizophrenia and related subjects* (pp. 284–303). New York: International Universities Press. [Reprinted London: Karnac Books, 1986.]

Searles, H. F. (1987). *Countertransference and Related Subjects*. Madison, Connecticut: International Universities Press, Inc.

Segal, H. (1957). Notes on symbol formation. *International Journal of Psycho-Analysis, 38*: 391–397.

Segal, H. (1957). Notes on symbol formation. In: *The Work of Hannah Segal*. New York: Aronson.

Segal, H. (1979). *Klein*. London: Fontana/Collins.

Shakespeare, W. (1919) *Hamlet*. London: Methuen.

Sharpe, E. F. (1950). The technique of psycho-analysis—(2). The analysand. In: *Collected Papers on Psycho-Analysis*. London: Hogarth Press.

Shoenberg, P. J. (1975). The symptom as stigma or communication in hysteria. *International Journal of Psychoanalytic Psychotherapy, 4*: 507–518.

Shoenberg, P. J. (1986). The psychotherapist's anxiety about bodily processes and some ways in which this anxiety may effect the long term psychotherapy of psychosomatic disorders. In: J. H. Lacey & D. A. Sturgeon (Eds.),. *Proceedings of the 15th Conference on Psychosomatic Research* (pp. 54–58). London: John Libby.

Shoenberg, P. J. (1991). Psychosomatic Disorders. In: J. Holmes (Ed.), *Textbook of Psychotherapy in Psychiatric Practice, Chap. 16* (pp. 383–394). London: Churchill Livingston.

Sinason, M. (1993). Who is the mad voice inside? *Psychoanalytic Psychotherapy, 7* (3): 207–221.

Sophocles. (1994). *Oedipus The King*. Translated by David Grene. Random House, U.K.: Everyman Library.

Spence, D. Narrative persuasion. *Psychoanalysis and Contemporary Thought, 6*: 457–482.

Stanton, M. (1990). *Sandor Ferenczi*. London: Free Association Books.

Steiner, J. (1985). Turning a blind eye: the cover up for Oedipus. *International Review of Psychoanalysis, 12*: 161–172.

Steiner, J. (1993). *Psychic Retreats*. London: Routledge.

Stern, D. (1974). Mother and infant at play; the dyadic interaction involving facial, vocal and gaze behaviours. In: M. Lewis & L. A. Rosenblum (Eds.), *The Effect of the Infant on its Caregiver*. New York: John Wiley & Sons.

Stern, D. et al. (1998). Non-interpretive mechanisms in psychoanalytic psychotherapy. *International Journal of Psychoanalysis, 79*: 903–321.

Strachey, J. (1934). The nature of the therapeutic action of psychoanalysis. *International Journal of Psychoanalysis, 15*: 127–159.

Sutherland, J. D. (1989). *Fairbairn's Journey into the Interior*. London: Free Association Books.

Symington, N. (1988). The analyst's act of freedom. In: G. Kohon (Ed.), *The British School of Psychoanalysis: The Independent Tradition*. London: Free Association Books.

Taylor, G. J., Bagby, R. M., & Parker, J. D. A. (1997). *Disorders of Affect Regulation* (pp. 1–6, 26–46, 114–138). Cambridge: Cambridge University Press.

Temperley, J. (1984). Settings for psychotherapy. *British Journal of Psychotherapy, 1* (2): 101–111.

The ICD-10 Classification of Mental and Behavioural Disorders. (1992). World Health Organisation.

Tomkins, S. S. (1962). *Affect/Imagery/Consciousness: Vol. 1. The Positive Affects*. New York: Springer.

Tomkins, S. S. (1963). *Affect/Imagery/Consciousness: Vol. 2. The Negative Affects*. New York: Springer.

Tomkins, S. S. (1995). *Exploring Affect*. Cambridge University Press.

Viederman, M. (1991). The real person of the analyst and his role in the process of analytic cure. *Journal of the American Psychoanalytic Association, 39*: 451–489.

Wigoder, D. (1987). *Images of Destruction*. London: Routledge & Kegan Paul.

Winnicott, D. W. (1949). The baby as a going concern. In: *The Child the Family and the Outside World*. London: Penguin.

Winnicott, D. W. (1951). Critical notice of on not being able to paint. In: C. Winnicott, R. Shepherd & M. Davies (Eds.), *Psychoanalytic Explorations* (1990). London: Karnac Books.

Winnicott, D. W. (1954). Metapsychological and clinical aspects of regression within the psycho-analytic set-up. In: *Collected Papers: Through Paediatrics to Psycho-Analysis*. London: Tavistock, 1958. [Reprinted London: Karnac Books, 1992.]

Winnicott, D. W. (1958). The capacity to be alone. In: *The Maturational Processes and the Facilitating Environment*. London: Hogarth Press and the Institute of Psycho-Analysis (1965).

Winnicott, D. W. (1962). The aims of psycho-analytical treatment. In: *The Maturational Processes and the Facilitating Environment*. London: Hogarth, 1965. [Reprinted London: Karnac Books, 1985.]

Winnicott, D. W. (1965). The concept of trauma in relation to the development of the individual within the family. In: C. Winnicott, R. Shepherd & M. Davis (Eds.), *Psycho-Analytic Explorations*. London: Karnac Books, 1989.

Winnicott, D. W. (1968). The use of an object and relating through identifications. In: *Playing and Reality* (1980). Harmondsworth: Penguin.

Winnicott, D. W. (1974). Fear of Breakdown. *International Review of Psycho-analysis, 1* (1&2).

Winnicott, D. W. (1989, 1964). Psycho-somatic illness in its positive and negative aspects. In: C. Winnicott, R. Shepherd & M. Davies (Eds.), *Psychoanalytic Explorations* (pp. 103–115). London: Karnac Books.

Winnicott, D. W. (1989, 1968). Interpretation in psychoanalysis. In: C. Winnicott, R. Shepherd & M. Davies (Eds.), *Psychoanalytic Explorations* (pp. 103–115). London: Karnac Books.

Wolff, H. H. (1990). In: H. Wolff, A. Bateman & D. Sturgeon (Eds.), *UCH Textbook of Psychiatry, Chap. 16* (pp. 159, 184–186, 201). London: Duckworth.

Wolff, H. H., & Shoenberg, P. J. (1990). Psychosomatic aspects of individual disorders, Chap. 38. In: H. Wolff, A. Bateman & D. Sturgeon (Eds.), *UCH Textbook of Psychiatry* (pp. 440–484). London: Duckworth.

Yung, A. R., & McGorry, P. D. The prodromal phase of first-episode psychosis: past and current conceptualizations. *Schizophrenia Bulletin, 22* (2): 353–370.

INDEX

and money, 3, 72, 78
naturalness in, *see* naturalness
and real relationship, 32
responsibility of, 184
"tease" of, 183
and touch, 2, 20–21, 27
and transference, 17, 35
anger, expressing, 112, *see also*
  aggressive behaviour; violence
Anna O (patient), 9
anorexia, 151
anxiety
  defences, 167
  physical effects of, 102, 105–6, 168,
    see also somatic symptoms
  in psychosis, 120
  separation, *see* separation anxiety
  stranger, 144
Archer, S., 4, 137–52
Argentina, psychoanalysis in, 29
assault, *see* aggressive behaviour;
  violence
asthma, 102, 105, 154
attention, evenly suspended, 31, 40
Auerhahn, N. C., 56

back pain, 106
Baby as a Going Concern, 67
Baker, R., 66, 67, 68, 74
Balint, M., 74, 153, 164
Bauman, Z., 184
Becker, Ernest, 82
Bergler, E., 38
Berkowitz, R., 3, 59–68, 73
Berman, I., 122
Bion, W. R.
  on containment, 8, 11, 12, 37, 167
  on pleasure/frustration, 60, 61,
    62, 65, 66
  on psychosis, 118, 122, 128, 130,
    131
Bleger, J., 10
Bollas, C., 47, 48, 49, 52
Booth, W. C., 43, 44, 45, 46, 51
borderline personality disorder, 2,
  45, 52, 129

boundaries, therapeutic, 9–12, 16, 19
  and naturalness, 18, 19, 20–25, 29
  and setting, analytic, 9, 10, 11, 12
  and touch, 2, 20–21, 27
Bowlby, J., 168
Brafman, A. H., 4, 153–64
brain structure/function, 144–45
  changes, with psychotherapy,
    124–25
breaks, from therapy, 3, 165–76
  and separation anxiety, 165–76
breathing difficulties,
  psychosomatic, 105–6, 112
Brenman, E., 169
Breuer, J., 8, 9, 116
Brighton Rock, 45–46
British Objects Relations School, 127
Britton, R. S., 75
bronchial asthma, 102, 105, 154
Bryher, I., 20
Buie, D. H., 156, 157
bullying, 46, 57

Campbell, D., 155, 157
Carpy, Denis V., 63
Carroll, L., 43, 52
Casement, P., 23, 62
cathartic method, 8
CFS (chronic fatigue syndrome), 102
change, psychic, 3, 11, 18, 175
  and brain structure/function,
    124–25
  and narrative, 51, 56
  resistance to, 86, 87
  and shame, 152
  and transference, 16–17, 175
charges, *see* money
Chasseguet-Smirgel, J., 140, 141, 151
child psychotherapy, 17
childhood environment, failure of,
  90, 92, 97, 99
  analysing, 11
  and suicide, 155, 158, 162, 163
chronic fatigue syndrome (CFS), 102
*Classification of Mental and
  Behavioural Disorders*, 119